Leopold George Gordon Robbins

The Devolution of Real Estate on Death

Under Part 1 of the Land Transfer Act, 1897

Leopold George Gordon Robbins

The Devolution of Real Estate on Death
Under Part 1 of the Land Transfer Act, 1897

ISBN/EAN: 9783337159146

Printed in Europe, USA, Canada, Australia, Japan

Cover: Foto ©ninafisch / pixelio.de

More available books at **www.hansebooks.com**

THE

𝔇evolution of 𝔑eal 𝔈state

ON DEATH,

UNDER

PART I.

OF THE

LAND TRANSFER ACT, 1897.

WITH THE ACT AND RULES.

BY

LEOPOLD GEORGE GORDON ROBBINS,

Of Lincoln's Inn, Barrister-at-Law; Reader in Equity to the Inns of Court.

LONDON

BUTTERWORTH & CO., 7, FLEET STREET, E.C.
Law Publishers.

1898.

LONDON:
PRINTED BY SHAW AND SONS, FETTER LANE AND CRANE COURT, E.C.

PREFACE.

PART I. of the Land Transfer Act, 1897 (60 & 61 Vict. c. 65), consisting of five sections only, seems to affect as many important changes in the law of real property. No doubt, it was hopeless at the end of the last Session of Parliament, having regard to the pressure of other business, to attempt to pass an Act altering the law relating to the devolution of real estate on death, and containing well considered and clearly expressed provisions dealing specifically and positively with the many questions of doubt and difficulty which must otherwise necessarily arise by reason of such material alteration of an ancient and complicated system. Such provisions must have called attention to the important character of the proposed alterations, and would in all probability have aroused such serious opposition, perhaps to the principle, or, at all events, to matters of detail, so as to destroy all chance of passing the Act, at all events except by the sacrifice of Part I. The prospect of carrying into effect a legal reform of great importance and usefulness, in the opinion of many jurists and politicians, no doubt fully justified, in the eyes of the supporters of that reform, the tacking of these few and concisely worded sections to an Act with which they have no essential or very apparent connection.

The qualities of brevity and simplicity which characterize these five sections, however, are obtained as an inevitable sacrifice of completeness and clearness; and, accordingly, an attentive perusal of this Part of the Act raises in the mind of any reader acquainted with the law of real property numerous questions, to the solution of which the language of the Act affords little or no guidance, and which he must accordingly solve to the best of his ability and judgment, at some risk to his clients, or submit to the decision of the Court.

The principal changes which this Part of the Act effects, or seems to effect, are as follows:—

(1.) "Real estate" of a deceased owner is made to vest on the death in his personal representatives, instead of, as heretofore, in the devisee or heir; but this Act contains no definition of "real estate" (other than an exception of copyholds and customary lands), and it is thus far from clear what kinds of real property are intended so to vest, or what quality or quantity of estate the personal representatives are intended to take.

(2.) The same or the like powers, rights, duties, and liabilities are conferred and imposed on personal representatives in respect of real estate as they now have in respect of personal estate; they may thus obtain probate or administration of real estate, deal with real estate before probate or administration, sell or mortgage real estate for purposes of administration, and manage the property while retained by them for such purposes; but these powers, etc., are stated not specifically and in detail, but only generally and by reference, and subject to the qualifications that they are to apply to real estate "so far as the same are applicable," and that personal representatives are to hold such property as "trustees"; judicial decision can alone solve the questions which must arise as to the import and extent of these qualifications.

(3.) Real estate is rendered legal assets for payment of debts in the hands of personal representatives *virtute officii* independently of any charge thereon of debts contained in a will, instead of as heretofore merely equitable assets in the hands of the devisee or heir.

(4.) Real estate is to be administered "with the same incidents, as if it were personal estate," without qualification. The effect of these words, coupled with other incidental provisions of the Act, is apparently to render real estate liable to payment of legacies[*]; but this change in the law, if effected, is left to inference, and not positively and distinctly enacted. Moreover, there is no express saving of the rights of an heir in case of intestacy, and it is also left to inference that the intention and effect of the Act is not to disturb those rights, except so far as the real estate is required for purposes of administration; but, as distribution of residue not so required is one of the "incidents" of personal estate, it might have been better if all doubt on this point had been dispelled by positive enactment.

Since the remarks in the text (pp. 92, 93), were through the press an objection was made to the views there expressed, on the ground that the last clause of section 2 (3) of the Act of 1897 negatives the liability of real estate to debts by virtue of this Act. But the writer submits that this is not the effect of the clause, which merely preserves the right of a testator to charge legacies on land generally or specifically, so as to render the land so charged liable to legacies primarily, or out of the order in which it otherwise would be liable by virtue of the Act.

(5.) Real estate, on completion of the administration, or if and so far as not required for purposes of administration, is to be transferred to the persons entitled thereto by assent or conveyance. No form of assent is prescribed by the Act (except for the purpose of obtaining registration), and accordingly the beneficial interest in realty, if not the legal estate, may in some cases pass from one party to another without deed or any written instrument, or any formality such as the old livery of seisin, but by mere parol, or even without a word spoken between the parties, by some act of the personal representatives from which an assent may be implied.

This short statement of what the Act does, and omits to do, makes it obvious that many questions of doubt and difficulty will arise as to the construction and effect of the Act. In the following pages an attempt has been made to point out some of these questions, and, as far as possible, to solve or explain them, in the hope that the observations therein contained may be of service to the legal profession, when they have to consider the provisions of Part I. of the Act of 1897 (as many of them will very soon be called upon to do), and the changes thereby effected in the law as to the devolution of real estate on death, changes the nature and extent of which do not seem, so far, to have excited the attention which their importance deserves and must inevitably demand.

L. G. GORDON ROBBINS.

Lincoln's Inn,
  January 6th, 1898.

TABLE OF CONTENTS.

CHAPTER I.
INTRODUCTORY CHAPTER.
        PAGE
1. Of the law as to devolution of real estate and statutory modifications thereof ... 1
2. Of the Land Transfer Act, 1897, generally ... 5
3. General effect of Part I. of the Land Transfer Act, 1897 ... 7

CHAPTER II.
ESTABLISHMENT OF REAL REPRESENTATIVES.
1. General remarks ... 9
2. Real estate of testator vests in his executors ... 10
3. Real estate, if executors are not appointed or renounced, or in case of intestacy, vests in administrators ... 14
4. At what time real estate vests in executors or administrators ... 18

CHAPTER III.
WHAT ESTATES AND INTERESTS IN REALTY VEST IN REAL REPRESENTATIVES.
1. Legal and equitable "real estates" vest in personal representatives ... 20
2. Exception where right to take by survivorship ... 23
3. Exception of copyholds and customary freeholds ... 24
4. What estates and interests are real property vesting in executors and administrators ... 25
5. Appointment of real estates under general powers ... 35
6. What "real estate" will pass to executors or administrators... 37
7. As to shifting uses, executory devises, and contingent remainders ... 49

CHAPTER IV.
OF THE NATURE AND EXTENT OF THE INTEREST IN REAL ESTATE TAKEN BY EXECUTORS AND ADMINISTRATORS.
1. Nature of the interest ... 52
2. Duration of the interest in realty taken by personal representatives ... 59

CHAPTER V.

OF THE POWERS OF EXECUTORS AND ADMINISTRATORS IN RELATION TO REAL ESTATE.

		PAGE
1.	General enactment as to powers, etc., of personal representatives	60
2.	Dealings with real estate before probate or grant of administration	61
3.	Powers of executors and administrators to sell or mortgage real estate	64
4.	Powers of executors and administrators as to leasing and management of real estate during period of administration	75

CHAPTER VI.

RIGHTS, DUTIES, AND LIABILITIES OF PERSONAL REPRESENTATIVES IN RESPECT OF REAL ESTATE.

1.	Duty of personal representatives is to pay debts and deliver property so far as not required for such payment to the persons entitled thereto	82
2.	Liability of personal representatives for their acts and defaults in administering real estate	86

CHAPTER VII.

APPLICATION OF ESTATE IN THE ADMINISTRATION OF THE ASSETS OF A DECEASED PERSON.

1.	General statutory rule as to administration of real estate	90
2.	Payment of legacies out of real estate	92
3.	Order of application of assets in administration	93
4.	Effect of the Act on the distinction between legal and equitable assets	94

CHAPTER VIII.

TRANSFER TO DEVISEE OR HEIR.

1.	Assent to devises	99
2.	Right of devisees and heirs to compel conveyance	109

CHAPTER IX.

APPROPRIATION OF REAL ESTATE TO LEGACIES, ETC. 112

CHAPTER X.

MISCELLANEOUS MATTERS.

1.	Registration of proprietorship of real estate	116
2.	Stamp duties	118
3.	Liability to succession and estate duties	119

APPENDIX.

Land Transfer Act, 1897 (60 & 61 Vict. c. 65)	121
Provisional Land Transfer Rules	129

TABLE OF CASES.

	PAGE
Adair v. Shaw	59
Adams v. Pierce	101, 102
Andrews v. Wingley	65
Angier v. Stannard	111
Anon	87
Att.-Gen. v. Geary	79
Att.-Gen. v. Owen	77
Austin v. Beddoe	102
Ayres, Re	104
Bacon v. Simpson	63
Bailey v. Appleyard	46
Bailey v. Ekins	97
Bailey v. Stevens	46
Bain v. Sadler	96
Balfour v. Cooper	65
Ball v. Hains	69
Ball v. Harris	65
Barber, Re	87
Barker v. Barker	80
Barker v. Devonshire (Duke of)	74
Barker v. May	97
Barnard v. Pomfret	107
Barrett v. Hartley	87
Bastard v. Stukeley	101
Bate, Re	93
Bath (Earl of) v. Bradford (Earl of)	68
Becket v. Bradley	77
Bedingfield, Re	87
Blackborough v. Davis	59
Bleazard v. Whalley	79
Bolles v. Nyseham	100
Booth v. Booth	86
Bosworth, Re	89
Brackenbury, Re	17
Braithwaite, Re	113
Brazier v. Hudson	62, 104
Bridge v. Brown	79
Brocksopp v. Barnes	87
Bromley v. Wright	113
Buckeridge v. Ingram	45
Buckley v. Howell	72
Burgess v. Robinson	113

	PAGE
Butler, Re	94
Buttonshaw v. Martin	111
Buxton v. Buxton	87
Byrchall v. Bradford	114
Caldecott v. Brown	79
Chaffe v. Kelland	111
Chamberlain v. Chamberlain	102
Charitable Corporation v. Sutton	87
Cholmley v. Paxton	72
Clay and Tetley's Contract, Re	67
Clay v. Willis	97
Claydon v. Green	21
Clegg v. Rowland	77
Clitheroe, Re	56
Cochrane v. Robinson	84
Cole v. Miles	101, 103, 109
Colyer v. Finch	65
Conro v. Conro	65
Const v. Harris	100
Constable v. Nicholson	46
Cook v. Gregson	94, 97
Cooke v. Loxley	77
Coombs v. Coombs	17
Cooper, Re	65
Coppin v. Coppin	106
Corsellis, Re	87
Cowin, Re	88
Cowley v. Wellesley	80
Cray v. Willis	109
Cull, Re	111
Cuthbertson v. Irving	77
Davey v. Durrant	72
Davey v. Thornton	111
Davies v. Nicholson	82
Davis v. Davis	106
Davis v. Dysart	88
Davis v. Harforde	77
Dean v. Allen	84
Delancy v. Fox	77
Devon (Duke of) v. Atkins	105
Doe v. Glen	63

TABLE OF CASES.

	PAGE
Doe r. Guy	101
Doe r. Huntington	41
Doe r. Hughes	65
Doe r. Maberley	107
Doe r. Shotter	64
Doe r. Sturgess	103
Doe r. Tatchell	107
Dover, Ex parte	114
Downs r. Grazebrook	72
Drake r. Trefusis	79
Drybutter r. Bartholomew	45
Duke r. Ricks	66
Dunman, Ex parte	72
Easton r. Pratt	77
Eglin r. Sanderson	88
Elias r. Snowdon Slate Co.	80
Elliot r. Dewsley	64
Elliot r. Merryman	64
Elwell r. Quast	111
Elwood r. Christy	62
England r. Tredegar	84
Fairland r. Percy	81
Fell r. Lutwidge	63
Fenton r. Clegg	62, 104
Fitzpatrick r. Waring	76
Flanders r. Clark	13, 103
Fleming r. Buchanan	68
Fleming r. Richardson	36
Frazer r. Murdock	115
Freeman r. Fairlie	88
Fry r. Tapson	73
Garland, Ex parte	80, 81
Gaskin r. Rogers	113
Gawler r. Standerwick	113
George r. Hillbanke	37
Gerrard r. Gerrard	46
Godfrey r. Watson	87
Goodson r. Ellison	111
Green r. Pigott	113, 115
Gresham r. Cotton	66
Greville r. Browne	64
Grey r. Mannock	34
Hall r. Carter	74
Hallet, Re	106
Hampshire r. Bradley	110
Harley, Ex parte	72
Hart r. Middlehurst	37
Hawker r. Saunders	107
Hawkins r. Day	83
Henderson r. McIver	88

	PAGE
Henry r. Macdonald	88
Hickling r. Boyer	84
Hill r. Gomme	83
Hill r. Simpson	74
Holdensby r. Spofforth	66
Holder r. Preston	70
Holford r. Phipps	111
Holkirk r. Holkirk	103
Holmes r. Coghier	37
Holt r. Winchester	44
Honeywood r. Honeywood	80
Hooper r. Clark	46
Hodgkinson r. Quinn	65
Horner r. Horner	63
Hudson r. Bell	73
Hughes r. Williams	87
Humphreys r. Ingledon	63
Hunt r. Stephens	62
Hyde r. Dallaway	73
Ithell r. Beane	74
Jeffcock, Re	77
Jenney r. Andrews	36
Johnson r. Mills	113
Jones, Re	56
Jones r. Lewis	110
Keating r. Lloyd	76
Kendall r. Russell	115
Kenrick r. Beauclerk (Lord)	65
Kilmurry (Lord) r. Geary	74
Kimberley r. Tew	115
Kirkman r. Booth	80
Knatchbull r. Fearnehead	83
Lambert's Estate, Re	16
Lampot's Case	100
Lang, Re	95
Langford r. Selmes	77
Lewis r. Freke	74
Lingard r. Derby (Earl of)	68
Littleton r. Hibbins	98
Livesey r. Livesey	106
Longstaffe r. Fenwick	87
Macartney r. Blundell	77
Maclaren r. Stainton	79
M'Leod r. Drummond	65
Maggi, Re	95
Mannox r. Greener	65
Marsden, Re	59, 86
Marsh r. Russell	106
Martin r. Fuller	63
Mason, Re	88

TABLE OF CASES.

xiii

	PAGE
Mason v. Farnell	109
Massingberd's Settlement, Re...	114
Mead v. Lord Ossery	65, 106
Metcalf v. Hutchinson	65
Metters v. Brown	63
Mills v. Banks	65
Moore v. Frowd	87
Morgan, Re	56
Morgan v. Thomas	63
Morley v. Cook	73
Mucklow v. Fuller	86
Moses v. Levy	63
Nairn v. Majoribanks	79
Naylor v. Arnett	76
New v. Jones	88
Newton, Re	17
Newton v. Askew	88
Newton v. Metropolitan Rail.	62
Noel v. Robinson	106
Norman v. Baldry	83
Northey v. Northey	100
Oceanic Steam Co. v. Sutherbury	77
Orr v. Kaimes	106
Owen v. Delamere	81
Page v. Cooper	65
Passmore v. Yardley	107
Payne v. Barker	110
Pears v. Lacy	46
Pearse v. Green	88
Pearson v. Archdeaken	83
Peirce v. Scott	66
Pennell v. Deffell	106
Penny v. Penny	98
Pharmaceutical Society v. London, etc., Supply Association	77
Phillips v. Hartley	63
Phillips v. Munnings	114
Phipps v. Annesley	113
Pilling's Trusts, Re	19
Pinchon's case	53
Pinney v. Pinney	104
Postlethwaite, Re	88
Powys v. Blagrave	88
Prince's Case	104
Pullen v. Smith	113
Rakestraw v. Brewer	19
Rector v. Gennet	83
Rex or Reg. v. Shingle	44
Rex v. Stone	62, 104

	PAGE
Rex v. Tolpuddle	38
Rex v. Wade	97
Rhodes v. Brown	83
Richards v. Brown	103
Richardson, Ex parte	81
Richardson v. Gifford	109
Ripley v. Waterworth	2
Robinson v. Lowater	64
Robinson v. Pett	87
Rock v. Hardman	115
Roe v. Summersett	62
Rowley v. Adams	87
Ryder v. Bickerton	88
Salaman v. Sopwith	77
Salt, Re	94
Saunder's Case	100
Scott v. Tyler	69
Sevin v. Okeley	97
Sharp v. Lush	98
Shaw, Re	76
Shaw v. Bonner	65
Sherwood v. Winchcombe	44
Sibley v. Perry	113
Sitwell v. Bernhard	115
Smith v. Day	83
Smith v. Morgan	95
Speight v. Gaunt	87
Spode v. Smith	82
Spon v. Smith	106
Stevenson v. Mayor of Liverpool	102
Stokes, Re	94
Stronghill v. Austen	64
Stott v. Milne	111
Stubb's Estate, Re	95
Sutton v. Sutton	21
Talbot v. Marshfield	88
Tanqueray-Willaume and Landau, Re	74, 91
Tarn v. Commercial Bank of Sydney	62
Thirby v. Yeats	111
Thompson v. Hardinge	24
Townson v. Tickell	104
Tremere v. Morrison	79
Turner, Re	89
Truscott v. Diamond Rock Boring Co.	77
Underwood v. Trower	89
Van Hagan, Re	68
Venn and Furze's Contract, Re	91
Vilk v. Brime	97

	PAGE
Wade v. Marsh	78
Waldo v. Waldo	80
Walker, Re	114
Wankford v. Wankford	18, 62
Ward v. Grey	113
Waters, Re	115
Watkins v. Cheek	74
Weall, Re	87
Webb v. Adkins	62
Webb v. Jones	114
Webb v. Needham	17
Webber v. Lee	46
Webber v. Webber	113
Westwick v. Wyers	106
Whistler, Re	91
White v. Cuddon	72
Whitehead v. Taylor	62
Whiteley, Re, Whiteley v. Learoyd	87
Williams v. Lomas	36
Williams v. Nixon	86
Williams v. Williams	27
Williams' Estate, Re	95
Williams' Trusts	19
Willis v. Hiscox	110
Wilson v. Fielding	95
Wood v. Patteson	76, 77
Wood v. Richardson	72
Wooldridge v. Bishop	63
Wragg v. Denham	87
Wroe v. Seed	88
Wynne v. Humberston	88
Young v. Holmes	103

TABLE OF STATUTES.

		PAGE
13 Edw. 1, c. 1	(Fines and Recoveries : Land (entail))	34
21 Hen. 8, c. 4	(Administration of Estates)	70
27 Hen. 8, c. 10	(Statute of Uses)	1, 49
32 Hen. 8, c. 1	(Will)	1
c. 7	(Tithes)	44
34 Hen. 8, c. 5	(Wills)	1
22 & 23 Car. 2, c. 10	(Statute of Distribution)	16
29 Car. 2, c. 3	(Statute of Frauds)	1, 34, 35
3 Will. & M. 14	(Fraudulent Devises)	67
14 Geo. 2, c. 20	(Common Recoveries, etc.)	34
17 Geo. 2, c. 38	(Poor Relief Act, 1743), s. 3	98
57 Geo. 3, c. 29	(Trade, America, etc.), s. 51	98
1 Will. 4, c. 47	(Debts Recovery)	67
3 & 4 Will. 4, c. 42	(Civil Procedure Act, 1833)	78
c. 74	(Fines and Recoveries Act, 1833)	32
c. 104	(Administration of Estates Act, 1833)	68
1 Vict. c. 26	(Wills Act, 1837)	1, 2, 34, 36, 48
12 & 13 Vict. c. 106	(Bankruptcy)	43
16 & 17 Vict. c. 51	(Succession Duty Act, 1853)	118
20 & 21 Vict. c. 77	(Court of Probate Act, 1857)	14
22 & 23 Vict. c. 35	(Law of Property Amendment Act, 1859)	66, 72, 83
32 & 33 Vict. c. 46	(Administration of Estates Act, 1869)	69, 95, 98
36 & 37 Vict. c. 66	(Supreme Court of Judicature Act, 1873)	14
37 & 38 Vict. c. 78	(Vendor and Purchaser Act, 1874)	3
38 & 39 Vict. c. 60	(Friendly Societies Act 1875), s. 15	98
c. 77	(Supreme Court of Judicature Act, 1875)	69, 95
c. 87	(Land Transfer Act, 1875)	3
ss. 4, 11		117
40 & 41 Vict. c. 33	(Contingent Remainders Act, 1877)	50
44 & 45 Vict. c. 41	(Conveyancing and Law of Property Act, 1881)	3, 10, 18, 24, 33, 45, 72, 73
45 & 46 Vict. c. 38	(Settled Land Act, 1882)	28, 29, 56, 57
c. 75	(Married Women's Property Act, 1882)	104
46 & 47 Vict. c. 52	(Bankruptcy Act, 1883)	30
52 & 53 Vict. c. 7	(Customs and Revenue Act, 1889)	118
c. 53	(Paymaster General Act, 1889)	38
53 & 54 Vict. c. 69	(Settled Land Act, 1890)	28
54 & 55 Vict. c. 39	(Stamp Act, 1891) (Sched.)	117
56 & 57 Vict. c. 53	(Trustee Act, 1893)	70, 71
57 & 58 Vict. c. 30	(Finance Act, 1894)	119
59 & 60 Vict. c. 35	(Judicial Trustees Act, 1896)	89
60 & 61 Vict. c. 65	(Land Transfer Act, 1897), s. 3 (1)	116, 117, 118

Devolution of Real Estate
UNDER PART I. OF THE
LAND TRANSFER ACT, 1897.

CHAPTER I.
INTRODUCTORY CHAPTER.

1. OF THE LAW AS TO DEVOLUTION OF REAL ESTATE AND STATUTORY MODIFICATIONS THEREOF.

By the common law of England, upon the death of an owner of an estate of inheritance in fee simple his lands devolved upon his heir-at-law, and no testamentary disposition of the land was allowed (*a*). The land might, however, have been conveyed by the owner in his lifetime to another person to the uses of his will, and, in equity, the use of the land might have been disposed of by will, and in case of such devise the feoffee was deemed to hold the land to the use of the devisee, who was thus enabled to enjoy the beneficial interest in the land (*b*). *Devolution of real estate on heir by common law.*

The Statute of Uses (*c*) for a time destroyed this power of testamentary alienation; but, this being found inconvenient, by successive enabling statutes (*d*), and ultimately by the Wills Act (*e*), owners of real estate were enabled to devise the same at their free will and pleasure. *Statutes enabling devises of real estate.*

Personal estate, including chattels real, however, has always devolved, and still does devolve, upon the death *Devolution of personal estate.*

(*a*) Co. Litt. 111 C.
(*b*) 1 Saund. Uses 64. See Wright's Tenures, 172, 174.
(*c*) 27 Hen. 8, c. 10.
(*d*) 32 Hen. 8, c. 1; 33 Hen. 8, c. 5; 29 Car. II. c. 3.
(*e*) 1 Vict. c. 26, s. 3.

Chap. I.

of its owner, upon the executors named in his will, or, if there be none such, or if the executors so named renounce probate, or if the owner died without leaving any will, then upon his administrators duly constituted by letters of administration (*f*).

Statutory modifications of law of devolution of real estate.

It has long been the desire of many law reformers to assimilate the devolution of real and personal estate. It is not here intended to discuss the question of policy whether, and if so, how far such assimilation is desirable, but it may be useful and interesting to trace shortly the history of the gradual taking away from the heir and giving to personal representatives of a deceased person particular kinds of real estate by successive enactments.

Estate pur autre vie devolves on personal representatives in certain cases by Wills Act.

In an early case (*g*), where an estate *pur autre vie* in freeholds was limited to his executors, administrators and assigns, it was contended on behalf of the heir-at-law that the estate ought to be considered as realty and devolve accordingly; but it was held that where an estate *pur autre vie* in freeholds (*h*) was limited to the grantee and his executors or administrators, it was taken by his executors or administrators, according as he died testate or intestate, and was applicable and distributable as part of his personal estate. And by the Wills Act (*i*) (repealing previous enactments respecting *pur autre vie*) testamentary power was given over such estates of any tenure, whether corporeal or incorporeal; and it was provided that if no such disposition should be made, any such estate should be assets in the hands of the heir, if it should come to him by reason of special occupancy; but if there should be no special occupant, such estates should go to the executor or administrator of

---

(*f*) Williams' Executors.
(*g*) *Ripley* v. *Waterworth*, 7 Ves. 425.
(*h*) See *post* p. 33, as to whether estates *pur autre vie* are within the operation of the Land Transfer Act, 1897.
(*i*) 1 Vict. c. 26, ss. 3, 6.

the grantee, and should be assets in his hands, and be applied and distributed as personal estate.

By the Vendor and Purchaser Act, 1874 (*k*), the personal representatives of the mortgagee of real estate might on payment of the mortgage moneys convey the legal estate of the mortgage property (*l*); and by the same Act, upon the death of a bare trustee seised in fee simple his estate was made to vest like a chattel real in his executor or administrator (*m*); but this last enactment has been since repealed by the next mentioned Act.

By the Land Transfer Act, 1875 (*n*), upon the death of the proprietor of a charge registered under that Act, his executor or administrator is entitled to be registered as proprietor in his place, thereby vesting in him the power of dealing with the mortgage by way of transfer or reconveyance by entry on the register without any need for the concurrence of the devisee or heir to pass the legal estate.

By the same Act, section 5 of the Vendor and Purchaser Act is repealed, and in lieu thereof it is enacted that upon the death of a bare trustee intestate, as to any corporeal or incorporeal hereditaments of which such trustee was seised in fee simple, such hereditaments not being land registered under this Act should vest like a chattel real in the legal personal representative from time to time of such trustee (*o*).

A more extended and important alteration in the law as to the devolution of real property was effected by section 30 of the Conveyancing and Law of Property Act, 1881 (*p*), which enacts as follows:—

(1.) Where an estate or interest of inheritance, or limited to the heir as special occupant, in any tene-

(*k*) 37 & 38 Vict. c. 78.
(*l*) Ib. s. 4.
(*m*) Ib. s. 5.
(*n*) 38 & 39 Vict. c. 87, s. 42.
(*o*) Ib. s. 48.
(*p*) 44 & 45 Vict. c. 41.

Chap. I.

ments or hereditaments, corporeal or incorporeal, is vested on any trust, or by way of mortgage, in any person solely, the same shall, on his death, notwithstanding any testamentary disposition, devolve to and become vested in his personal representatives or representative from time to time, in like manner as if the same were a chattel real vesting in them or him; and accordingly all the like powers, for one only of several joint personal representatives, as well as for a single personal representative, and for all the personal representatives together, to dispose of and otherwise deal with the same, shall belong to the deceased's personal representatives or representative from time to time, with all the like incidents, but subject to all the like rights, equities and obligations, as if the same were a chattel real vesting in them or him; and, for the purposes of this section, the personal representatives for the time being of the deceased shall be deemed in law his heirs and assigns, within the meaning of all trusts and powers.

(2.) Section 4 of the Vendor and Purchaser Act, 1874, and section forty-eight of the Land Transfer Act, 1875, are hereby repealed.

(3.) This section, including the repeals therein, applies only in cases of death after the commencement of this Act.

The effect of this enactment, which applies only in cases of death of a trustee or mortgagee since December 31st, 1881, is to vest the legal estate in realty subject to a trust or mortgage in the personal representatives of a deceased sole trustee or mortgagee, whether he died testate or intestate, and to render any devise of trust or mortgage estates unnecessary and inoperative. The beneficial interest in trust or mortgaged estates may, of course, still be bequeathed, but the legal estate in the mortgage property will pass to the personal representatives of the mortgagee notwithstanding such bequest.

A still greater advance towards the assimilation of the law of real and personal property has been introduced by Part I. of the Land Transfer Act, 1897, whereby, as will be seen hereafter, all the real estate (with certain exceptions) of a deceased person, whether testate or intestate, and notwithstanding any contrary disposition or direction in his will, is made to vest on his death in his executors or administrators for the purposes of the administration of his estate in like manner, and with the like powers of dealing with the same, as if it were a chattel real. *Land Transfer Act, 1897.*

In the Land Transfer Bill, 1888, were contained provisions assimilating the devolution on intestacy of the beneficial interest in real estate with that of personal estate, by making the real estate distributable in such a case among the next-of-kin of the intestate. But by the Act of 1897 real estate of a deceased person, whether testate or intestate, is vested, together with ancillary powers, in his executors or administrators for purposes of administration, and subject thereto as trustee for the devisee or (as it is conceived) the heir-at-law, or those claiming under them respectively, whose ultimate beneficial interest, subject to the requirements of administration, is thus, as it would seem, intended to be preserved. *Act does not alter ultimate devolution of beneficial interest in real estate.*

2. Of the Land Transfer Act, 1897, Generally.

The objects of the Land Transfer Act, 1897, as indicated by the title and preamble of the Act, are " to establish a Real Representative, and to amend the Land Transfer Act, 1875," therein referred to as " the principal Act." These two objects of the Act, carried into effect by the provisions therein contained, are both of great importance, but it is not obvious at first sight what connection they have with each other. The first object, that of creating a real representative, is the *General scope and objects of the Land Transfer Act, 1897.*

CHAP. I.

professed purpose of Part I. of the Act, containing five sections, which are the main subject for consideration in these notes. The remaining three parts of the Act, containing twenty-one sections, are devoted to the amendment and extension of the provisions of the Act of 1875 relating to the registration of title to land and dealings with lands so registered.

Connection between the the several parts of the Act.

The provisions of Parts II., III., and IV. of this Act appear to have been those to which the attention of the framers of the Act was especially directed, and to which primary importance was attached by the Legislature. But the establishment of a real representative must, no doubt, have been regarded as eminently desirable as ancillary to such primary object, in order to facilitate dealings with registered land. *Hæres nascitur non fit*; and it is obvious that the continuity of registration of land under the Land Transfer Acts might be seriously interfered with in cases of intestacy, if the heir-at-law should happen to be under disability, or out of the jurisdiction, or not to be found. Similar difficulties might, though no doubt less frequently, arise where real estate is devised. It is therefore, perhaps, not to be wondered at that the establishment of a real representive, at all events so far as relates to registered lands, should have been thought advisable in an Act to amend the Land Transfer Act, 1875, as forming part of and ancillary to the main provisions of such an Act.

Commencement of Act

The Land Transfer Act, 1897, comes into operation on January 1st, 1898 (*q*).

Short title.

This Act may be cited as the Land Transfer Act, 1897, and is to be construed as one with the principal Act, and that Act and this Act may be cited together as the Land Transfer Acts, 1875 and 1897.

(*q*) Section 25.

3. GENERAL EFFECT OF PART I. OF THE LAND TRANSFER ACT, 1897.

Part I. of this Act (sections 1, 5) purports to deal with the establishment of a real representative.

Real estate within the meaning of the Act belonging to a person dying after the commencement of the Act is to vest on his death in his personal representatives or representative, as if it were a chattel, and probate or letters of administration may be granted accordingly (*r*). *Vesting of real estate in personal representatives.*

Personal representatives in whom real estate is vested are to hold the estate as trustees for the person beneficially entitled thereto, with the same or the like powers and other powers generally, and subject to the same or the like obligations and liabilities, as are vested in or attached to the office of an executor or administrator of a chattel real (*s*). *Powers, etc., of personal representatives as to real estate.*

Personal representatives may at any time assent to the taking by a devisee, or convey to a devisee or heir, any land of a deceased owner which is not required for the general administration of his estate, and at the expiration of the year from the death of the owner, the devisee or heir may apply to the court to compel the personal representatives to convey the land to him, or, in the case of registered land, to cause him to be registered as proprietor of the land. No fees are to be chargeable on any transfer of registered land by personal representatives, unless for valuable consideration. On production of an assent in the prescribed form the registrar may register the person named therein as the proprietor of the land (*t*). *Assent and conveyance by personal representatives.*

The personal representatives of a deceased person may, after giving the prescribed notices, appropriate his real estate or any part thereof in or towards *Appropriation of real estate to legacies, etc.*

(*r*) Section 1.   (*s*) Section 2.   (*t*) Section 3.

CHAP. I.

satisfaction of a legacy or share in his residuary estate. A conveyance of real estate to the person to whom it is appropriated is to be liable to the same stamp duty as is payable on a like purpose. On production of the prescribed evidence of an appropriation the registrar may register the person to whom the property is appropriated as the proprietor of the land (*d*).

Liability of real estate to duty.

No higher or other duty is to be payable in respect of real estate than is now payable in respect thereof (*e*).

General application of Part I. of Act of 1897.

It will be observed that Part I. of the Act of 1897 is not confined in its operation to lands registered under the Act of 1875, or under that Act as amended by this Act, but is of general application, and introduces a complete change in the law as to the devolution of real estate within the meaning of the Act, belonging to any person who shall die on or after January 1st, 1898. The provisions of this part of the Act will receive a fuller and more detailed consideration in the following chapters.

(*u*) Section 4.   (*x*) Section 5.

CHAPTER II.

ESTABLISHMENT OF REAL REPRESENTATIVES.

1. GENERAL REMARKS.

THE full title of the Land Transfer Act, 1897, is "An Act to establish a Real Representative, and to amend the Land Transfer Act, 1875;" the preamble recites that "it is expedient to establish a real representative;" and at the commencement of Part I. of the Act appears a head-note in the words "Establishment of a Real Representative." But the expressions "real representative" or "real representatives" never occur elsewhere in this Part of the Act. *Title and preamble to Act of 1897.*

This Act, in fact, strictly speaking, does not establish a real representative at all. It does not authorize a testator to appoint a real representative by his will; and indeed, if a testator were to appoint one, not being a person appointed executor, as if a will were to say "I appoint A. and B. executors of this my will, and C. my real representative," it is conceived that the latter appointment would be nugatory, as being a testamentary disposition contravening the provision of the Act that real estate shall vest on death in the "personal representatives," *i.e.* the executors, and purporting to vest it in somebody else. Moreover, the Act does not give to the court any power to appoint a real representative as such, though the court is thereby empowered to grant probate or letters of administration to the personal representatives of a deceased person in respect of his real estate. *Act does not create "real representatives" as such.*

What this Act does enact is that (with certain exceptions to be hereinafter noticed) the real estate of a person dying on or after January 1st, 1898, shall vest in *Act vests real estate in personal representatives.*

CHAP. II.

his personal representatives or representative as if it were a chattel real. The personal representatives take, in their character as such, the real estate by virtue of the Act, as well as the personalty (if any) as heretofore by the general law.

Power to grant probate etc., as to realty, where no personalty.

By section 1 (3) of the Act, it is enacted that "probate and letters of administration may be granted in respect of real estate only, although there is no personal estate." Cases where there is absolutely no personal estate are not likely to be of frequent occurrence; but, in any such case, the person to whom probate or letters of administration are granted must apparently, by virtue of the grant, become a "personal representative," even though he has no personal estate to administer; otherwise nothing will vest in him by virtue of this Act. If, then, a person so appointed conveys by way of sale or mortgage, he will be able, by conveying "as personal representative," to give the statutory covenant against incumbrances implied by virtue of the Conveyancing and Law of Property Act, 1881 (*y*). Indeed, if he is to effectually give such a covenant, he must be expressed to convey "as personal representative," for the expression "real representative" does not occur either in the last-mentioned Act, or in the body of the Act of 1897, so that conveyance as such would be of no efficacy as importing any covenant for title.

2. REAL ESTATE OF TESTATOR VESTS IN HIS EXECUTORS.

If, then, a person dying on or after the 1st day of January, 1888, makes a will, and thereby appoints executors, his real estate must devolve by virtue of the Act on the executors so appointed, and on no other

(*y*) 44 & 45 Vict. c. 41. s. 7.

person, notwithstanding any disputation or direction to the contrary continued in the will.

It seems very doubtful whether it will be competent for a testator to appoint one set of executors in respect of his personal estate and another set of executors in respect of his real estate. Such separate appointments would, as it is conceived, amount to a testamentary disposition contrary to the Act. No doubt a testator may appoint special executors of a particular fund, and appoint general executors in respect of the remainder of his personal estate. But the power of appointing executors by will is founded upon principles of the Civil Law as recognised and adopted by the laws of England, and is not negatived or restricted, as regards the appointments of separate sets of executors by any statute, either expressly or by implication. The Act of 1897, however, says that the real estate of a deceased person is to vest "in his personal representatives or representative," which must apparently mean in all his representatives, if more than one. It is submitted that the appointment of separate "personal representatives" in respect of the real estate is impliedly prohibited by the Act, and that such separate appointment, if allowed, might be made the means of evading the provisions of the Act by the colourable use of the expression "personal representatives" in respect of the real estate as a description of the persons so appointed. Such persons would in effect be really "real representatives" independent of the personal representatives, strictly so called, or in other words, trustees with powers of sale, etc., either for the period of administration, if simply appointed executors in respect of the real estate, or permanently, if also made devisees in trust.

Such separate executors or trustees of the real estate would, assuming their appointments valid, have powers by virtue of this Act to sell or mortgage it for purposes

CHAP. II.

of administration, if they think fit to do so, and the real estate would be assets in their hands for payment of debts, etc. But if they should refuse to sell or mortgage on the ground that the personal estate primarily applicable for that purpose was not exhausted or otherwise, they could not be compelled by the executors of the personal estate to do so except by recourse to the court in an administration action as heretofore. The result of holding that separate executors of real estate may be appointed under this Act would thus seem to be to destroy the unity of administration apparently contemplated by this Act, and to leave matters in some cases pretty much as they were before; but it may be expected that this question will soon require and receive judicial determination.

The difficulty of advising, until a judicial decision on the point is obtained, as to how real estate devolves where separate sets of executors are appointed by will, will be much increased in cases where a testator appoints one set of executors of part of his personal estate, and another set of executors of the residue of his personal estate and of his real estate. In such a case it seems open to question whether the real estate must not vest by virtue of the Act in all the executors, special as well as general. If this is so, then the special executors will have cast upon them duties and responsibilities which the testator intended should not concern them. If otherwise, then it will be open to a testator by appointing executors of the bulk of his personal estate, and other special executors of a small and even illusory part of his personal estate and of his real estate, virtually to withdraw his real estate from the operation of the Act.

Result if only one set of executors may be appointed.

If the view above expressed is correct, that the appointment of separate sets of executors of personal estate and of real estate respectively is impliedly prohibited by the

Act, then the provision of the Act now under consideration may be productive in some cases of considerable inconvenience. If a testator desires to bequeath all his personalty to A., and to devise his real estate to B. absolutely, or to B. and C. upon trust for sale or upon other trusts, he must appoint A. and B., or A. B. and C. (as the case may be) general executors of his will, whereby the real estate and personal estate will alike vest in all of them; otherwise, if he appoints A. only executor, B., or B. and C., will take nothing until the administration of the general estate is completed, or until A. sooner assents to the devise; but the real estate will meanwhile vest in A., whose responsibility will be greatly increased beyond what the testator intended him to bear, by imposing upon him the duty of seeing that the real estate, with which he has presumably no beneficial concern, and with which he was intended to have no concern whatever, is properly administered. Conversely, if he makes B., or B. and C., executors as well as A., the personalty as well as the realty will vest in all the executors, and impose on B., or B. and C., the responsibility of seeing to the due administration of the personalty.

Where several executors are appointed they are all regarded in law as forming one person, and on the death of one of them, the office survives to the others or other (*z*). *Survival of office of executor.*

Upon the death of a sole executor, or of the survivor of several executors, in whom the real estate of a testator is vested by virtue of this Act, such real estate will vest like a chattel real in the executor of the will, if any, of the executors so dying (*a*) without having fully distributed the estate of his testator. *Executor of executor.*

(*z*) Williams on Executors (9th ed.) Vol. I., pp. 816, 821; see *Flanders* v. *Clarke*, 3 Atk. 509.

(*a*) Wentw. Off. Ex., pp. 462, 463; Williams on Executors (9th ed.) Vol. I., p. 204.

If, however, the executor should die intestate, his administrator cannot administer the estate of the original testator; accordingly, administration *de bonis non*, or whatever may be the corresponding form of administration prescribed in the case of real estate, must be granted to some person in order that the administration and distribution of the estate of the testator according to his will may be completed (*b*).

3. REAL ESTATE, IF EXECUTORS ARE NOT APPOINTED, OR RENOUNCE, OR IN CASE OF INTESTACY, VESTS IN ADMINISTRATORS.

If an owner of real estate dies not having appointed any executors of his will, or if all his executors renounce probate, or if he dies intestate, it will be necessary for some person or persons to apply to the court for letters of administration to the real estate *cum testamento annexo* or generally, as the case may require.

Application for letters of administration to real estate.

The application for letters of administration must be made in Principal Registry, or one of the District Registries, of the Probate Division of the High Court of Justice, which exercises, as successor of the old Court of Probate, "the voluntary and contentious jurisdiction and authority in relation to the granting or revoking probate of wills and letters of administration of the effects of deceased persons" (*c*). By the Judicature Act, 1873 (*d*), all causes and matters which would have been within the exclusive cognizance of the Court of Probate are assigned to the Probate Division. By the Land Transfer Act, 1897, the court is empowered to grant letters of administration in respect of real estate, although there is no personal estate (*e*).

(*b*) Shep. Touchstone 465; Williams on Executors (9th ed.), Vol. I. p. 204.

(*c*) See 20 & 21 Vict. c. 77, s. 4.
(*d*) 36 & 37 Vict. c. 66, s. 34.
(*e*) Section 1 (3) of this Act.

VESTING OF REAL ESTATE IN ADMINISTRATORS. 15

With regard to the persons who are entitled to apply for a grant of administration to the real estate of a deceased person, the Act of 1897, by section 2, sub-section (4), enacts as follows :—" Where a person dies possessed of real estate, the court shall, in granting letters of administration, have regard to the rights and interests of persons interested in his real estate, and his heir-at-law, if not one of the next-of-kin, shall be equally entitled to the grant with the next-of-kin, and provision shall be made by rules of court for adapting the procedure and practice in the grant of letters of administration to the case of real estate."

<small>Chap. II.

Right of heir to claim administration equally with next-of-kin.</small>

This enactment, and the rules to be made pursuant thereto, will operate in cases where a person dies possessed of real estate, either intestate, or without having appointed any executors of his will, where the executors named in the will refuse to prove it.

<small>Cases to which this enactment applies.</small>

With regard to personal estate, the statute 31 Ed. 3, statute 1, c. 11, provides that, in cases of intestacy, "the ordinary shall depute the next and most lawful friends of the dead person intestate to administer the goods." And by the statute 21 Hen. 8, c. 5, s. 3, it is provided that letters of administration may be granted to the widow of the deceased, or to the next of his kin, or to both, as by the discretion of the ordinary shall be thought good, and that, in case of claims made by several next-of-kin of equal degree, the ordinary is "to be at his election and liberty to accept any one or more making request." These statutes are still in force, and regulate the procedure and practice of the Probate Division of the High Court of Justice in granting letters of administration to personal estate.

<small>Rules as to person to whom administration of personal estate is granted</small>

It is further settled beyond question that a surviving husband has a paramount and exclusive right to administer the personal estate of his wife, either on

<small>Paramount claim of husband.</small>

Chap. II.

the ground that he is her "next and most lawful friend" within the meaning of the statute 31 Ed. 3, or by virtue of his marital rights at common law independently of statute (*f*); and this right is expressly confirmed by the statute 29 Car. 2, c. 3, which enacts that the Statute of Distributions (*g*) "shall not extend to the estates of *femes covert* that shall die intestate, but that their husbands may demand and have administration of their rights, credits, and other personal estates, and recover and enjoy the same as they might have done before the making of the said Act." The right is not taken away or in any way affected by the provisions of the Married Women's Property Act, 1882 (*h*). With regard to the claim of a husband to claim administration as to his wife's real estate, his rights as tenant by the curtesy must be borne in mind.

Next-of-kin, creditor, etc.

Subject to the rights of the husband to administration of the personal estate of his deceased wife, where a grant of administration is made *cum testamento annexo*, a legatee, or, if all decline, then a creditor or some other person is appointed administrator; administration under an intestacy is granted to one or more of the next-of-kin according to the nearness of their relationship to the deceased, or, if all decline, to a creditor or other nominee of the court.

Nature of heir's claim to administration.

It does not seem quite clear whether the provision in the Act of 1897 above set out that the "heir-at-law, if not one of the next-of-kin, shall be equally entitled to the grant with the next-of-kin," means that the heir is to be entitled as of right to a grant along with the next-of-kin, or with the surviving husband or widow, as the case may be; or whether it merely gives the heir a right to have his claims to administration of the

(*f*) Williams on Executors (9th ed.) 347.
(*g*) 22 & 23 Car. 2, c. 10.
(*h*) *Re Lambert's Estate*, 39 Ch. D. 626.

assets generally, real and personal, considered by the court on an equal footing with the claims of the next-of-kin, husband, or widow, thus leaving to the court the "election and liberty to accept" any one or more of the claimants as sole administrator of all the assets, to the exclusion of the heir, or of the next-of-kin, etc., if the court should so think fit.

As regards personal estates, the court has full power to make a grant to several persons either jointly over the whole assets, or separately by granting to them respectively several administrations of several parts of the estate (*i*). The court, as a general rule, leans strongly against joint administrations, unless with the consent of the persons claiming the grant (*k*). As regards real estates it would, no doubt, in many cases, be convenient if where an heir puts in a claim to administration along with the next-of-kin, the court should commit the administration of the real estate to the former, and that of the personal estate to the latter. But it may be doubted, on the grounds already stated, tending to negative the power of a testator to appoint a separate executor of his real estate, whether the court has jurisdiction under this Act to grant separate administrations as to the personalty to one person, and as to the realty to another person.

Whether the court has power to grant separate administrations, as to personalty to a next-of-kin, and as to realty to the heir.

A mortgagee or other creditor cannot obtain a grant of administration to personalty unless the next-of-kin refuses it (*l*). With regard to the administration of real estate, inasmuch as the heir is equally entitled to the grant with the next-of-kin, it is believed that a mortgagee or creditor will not be entitled to the grant unless both the heir and the next-of-kin refuse it.

Right of creditor to administration.

(*i*) Roll. Abr. tit. Executor (D.) pl. 1, p. 908.
(*k*) *Re Newton*, L. R. 1 P. & D. 285.
(*l*) *Webb* v. *Needham*, 1 Add. 494; see 2 Blackst. Comm. 505. See further as to grants of administration to creditor, *Coombs* v. *Coombs*, L. R. 1 P. & D. 272; *Re Brackenbury*, 2 P. D. 272.

CHAP. II.

Survival of office.

When administration is granted to several, and one dies, the office, with its incident duties and powers, survives to the others or other.

Determination of office by death of sole administrator.

The rights of an administrator cannot be transmitted, but are determined by his death. Accordingly, on the death of an administrator before he has completed the administration, and distributed the assets, a new administrator must be appointed (*m*).

---

4. AT WHAT TIME REAL ESTATE VESTS IN EXECUTORS OR ADMINISTRATORS.

Real estate devolves on executor from death of testator.

Where a testator appoints executors of his will, his real estate will devolve on them immediately on his death and before grant of probate, as has been and is the case as regards chattels real and other personalty.

Real estate devolves on administrator from grant of administration.

Where, however, this is not the case, then inasmuch as an administrator takes only by virtue of the grant of administration, and can do nothing as administrator before such grant (*n*), a question would seem to arise as to what becomes of the legal estate in the interval before the grant is made. A similar question arose on the construction of section 30 of the Conveyancing Act, 1881 (*o*), upon the death intestate of a sole surviving trustee. PEARSON, J., after pointing out that this Act provides that the legal estate in a trustee or mortgagee shall, on his death, devolve to and become vested in his personal representatives or representative from time to time, observed as follows:—"The question is, what happens when there is no personal representative?

(*m*) Shep. Touchst. 465; Williams on Executors, Part I., Bk. III., c. 4.
(*n*) *Wankford* v. *Wankford*, 1 Salk. 310. See Williams' Executors (9th ed.), Vol. 1, p. 342.
(*o*) 44 & 45 Vict. c. 41.

If the legal estate does not vest in the heir, where is it? On the other hand, the wording of the section seems to evince an intention to exclude the heir." But his lordship did not determine the question (*p*). It is obvious, however, that, even if the legal estate does vest in the heir pending the grant of letters of administration, no purchaser, mortgagee, or lessee could safely take from him a conveyance in fee or lease for a term, for the heir could only convey such estate as he has himself, which is determinable on the appointment of an administrator, upon whom not only the legal estate, but also the beneficial interest in the land, will devolve under this Act, with full powers of dealing therewith, in accordance with this Act, for purposes of administration.

(*p*) *Re Pilling's Trusts*, 26 Ch. D. 432. See *Rakestraw* v. *Brewer*, W. N. (1885), 73; 33 W. R. 559; *Re Williams Trusts*, 36 Ch. D. 231.

CHAPTER III.

WHAT ESTATES AND INTERESTS IN REALTY VEST IN REAL REPRESENTATIVES.

1. LEGAL AND EQUITABLE "REAL ESTATES" VEST IN PERSONAL REPRESENTATIVES.

Devolution of legal interest in real estate on death.

IT will be convenient in this place to set out *verbatim* the enactment whereby real estate within the meaning of the Act is made to devolve upon the executors or administrators of a deceased person. This enactment is as follows:—

> Section 1.—(1.) Where real estate is vested in any person without a right in any other person to take by survivorship it shall, on his death, notwithstanding any testamentary disposition, devolve to and become vested in his personal representatives or representative from time to time as if it were a chattel real vesting in them or him.

Legal estates in land of deceased persons devolve on their personal representatives.

It is clear that the effect of the above section as regards all cases coming within it, is to vest in the personal representatives of a deceased person all real estate within the meaning of the section to which he was beneficially entitled at law at the time of his death in like manner as a real chattel would hitherto have devolved, and still would devolve, on his executors or administrators. Thus, the estate of a man seised in fee simple of land free from incumbrances will now pass to his personal representatives; and if an owner of real estate within the meaning of the sub-section above set out, gives an equitable mortgage by agreement or deposit of deeds, but without parting with the legal estate to the mortgagee, such legal estate and also the beneficial interest subject to the mortgagee will, on the death of the mortgagor, devolve on his personal representatives, whether he dies intestate or purports to devise his estate immediately upon his death to any other person.

It will be observed that the marginal note to the above section mentions only the devolution of *legal* interest; but it is now settled, after some conflict of opinion, that the marginal notes to an Act of Parliament are not to be deemed part of the Act (*q*). Marginal notes to Acts of Parliament.

There appears, on an examination of the text of the statute, to be nothing which necessarily limits the application of Part I. to cases where the legal estate is vested in an owner of land at his death; and it is submitted that such restricted construction is inconsistent with the policy and spirit of the Act, which is evidently to assimilate for purposes of administration in cases falling within it, the law as to the devolution of real estate to that which has hitherto prevailed as regards personal estate. It is therefore conceived that the operation of the statute is not intended, and ought not to be regarded, as limited to cases where a deceased person had the legal estate in land vested in him at his death, but must be extended to cases where such estate was then outstanding in a trustee or mortgagee. Whether equitable interests in land are also within the Act.

It may then be assumed with some confidence that equitable, no less than legal estates in real estate, will by virtue of this Act pass, on the death of the owner, to his executors or administrators. And this being so, if the legal estate was outstanding in trustees upon trust for a person beneficially entitled in fee, as, for instance, if land was settled and all the particular estates having determined, the ultimate equitable remainder in fee vested in that person, he would have been entitled Legal estate outstanding in trustees for persons absolutely entitled.

(*q*) *Sutton* v. *Sutton*, 32 Ch. D. 511. See *Claydon* v. *Green*, L. R. 3 C. P. 511.

in his lifetime to call upon the trustees to convey the legal estate vested in them to him at any time. And, upon his death on or after January 1st, 1898, without having had the legal estate conveyed to him, the equitable estate or interest in the land and the right to compel conveyance by the trustees in whom it is vested will devolve upon the personal representatives of the deceased equitable owner.

Legal estate outstanding in a mortgagee.

Where an estate of inheritance in land is mortgaged, the equity of redemption is, until foreclosure, not merely a right of entry on payment of the mortgage moneys, but an estate vested in the mortgagor as owner of the land; and accordingly all incidents of ownership, including devolution and the right of devise, attached prior to the Act now under consideration to the mortgagor's estate, subject and without prejudice to the mortgage, but otherwise in like manner as if the land had not been in mortgage. It is conceived that this estate must now, on the mortgagor's intestacy or notwithstanding any contrary direction in his will, devolve by virtue of the present Act, in the first instance, upon his personal representatives, who will be entitled to retain it so long as is necessary for purposes of administration, and then will be compellable to vest it by assent or conveyance in the devisee named by the will, or in the heir-at-law, as the case may be.

The result then appears to be that, in the case of any person on or after January 1st, 1898, all his freehold estate of inheritance in any lands, no less than his chattels, both real and personal, will pass to his executors or administrators; and that no devise or testamentary direction to the contrary will be sufficient to oust their right; so that even a specific devisee will not be entitled to claim the land devised until the executors have assented to the devise.

2. Exception where Right to take by Survivorship.

Chap. III.

Section 1, sub-section (1), of the Act of 1897, excludes from the operation of the Act real estate vested in persons where there is a right in any other person to take by survivorship.

The class of cases which most obviously falls within this exception is that of estates in joint tenancy. Where an estate is given by deed or will to several persons, and their heirs or heirs and assigns, a joint tenancy is created, the legal effect of which is that the donees are collectively regarded as a single person; on the death of one or more of the component individuals making up that person, the others or other surviving take the whole of the estate between them or solely, as the case may be (*r*); and it is not till the death of the last survivor that this Act will come into operation and divert into the hands of the personal representatives of such survivor the property which, but for the Act, would have passed to his heir-at-law or devisee.

Joint tenants.

If the joint tenancy is severed by the disposal of his interest by a joint tenant, which he has full power to do by alienation *inter vivos*, but not by will, the unity of title will be destroyed, and a tenancy in common will be created, which will let in the operation of the Act (*s*).

The above remarks will apply equally to parceners, each of whom takes by right of survivorship on death of a co-parcener, and whose estates and interests are generally the same as those of joint tenants, except that as between co-parceners there is no unity of seisin, and that independently of statute, any one of

Co-parceners.

(*r*) Bac. Abr. tit. Joint Tenants A.); Co. Litt. 184 a.   (*s*) Co. Litt. 186 a.

them has always had the right to compel his co-owners to make partition (*t*).

Trustees of settlements and wills.

Where by a settlement created by deed or will, real estates are vested in trustees, the limitation is to them as joint tenants, and accordingly, upon the death of one of several trustees of real estate, the property will vest not in his personal representatives, but in the surviving trustees or trustee if any. Upon the death of a sole or last surviving trustee, the settled real estate will vest in his personal representatives by virtue of section 30 of the Conveyancing and Real Property Act, 1881 (*u*).

3. EXCEPTION OF COPYHOLDS AND CUSTOMARY FREEHOLDERS.

Exception of copyhold and customary lands.

By section 1 of the Act it is enacted as follows :—

(4.) The expression "real estate" in this part of this Act, shall not be deemed to include land of copyhold tenure or customary freehold in any case in which an admission or any act by the lord of the manor is necessary to perfect the title of a purchaser from the customary tenant.

Meaning of this sub-section.

This sub-section does not seem to be very happily worded; it seems to contemplate some classes of cases where admission, or some act of the lord, is not necessary to perfect the title of a purchaser from a customary tenant. But none such are to be found; "the great criterion of a customary estate is, that all alienations of it must be transacted, in part at least, in the lord's court" (*x*). The words after "customary freeholds" therefore appear to be surplusage, and might well have been omitted, as tending to make the

---

(*t*) Bac. Abr. tit. Co-parceners.
(*u*) 44 & 45 Vict. c. 41, set out *ante*, p. 3.
(*x*) *Thompson* v. *Hardinge*, 1 C. B. 940, and cases there cited; see Litt. 74, 75; see also *Delacherois* v. *Delacherois*, 11 H. L. C. at p. 83.

reader suppose that some lands of copyhold tenure or customary freehold are excluded, which seems not to be the case.

This exception from the operation of the Act of lands of copyhold or customary freehold tenure has the effect, in cases where such lands are in mortgage, of preserving the right of a mortgagee, who has not been admitted during the life of his mortgagor, to claim admission on the death of the mortgagor as against his customary heir or real representatives or any other person; and on the death of the mortgagee the right to admission vests in his personal representatives under section 30 of the Conveyancing and Real Property Act, 1881. Subject to the right of the mortgagee or his representatives to admission, the right vests in the devisee or customary heir of the mortgagor.

Saving thereby of mortgagee's right to admission on death of mortgagor.

---

4. WHAT ESTATES AND INTERESTS ARE REAL PROPERTY VESTING IN EXECUTORS AND ADMINISTRATORS.

The wording of section 1, sub-section (1), of the Act of 1897, does not seem to indicate the nature and extent of the estates and interests in real property, which are intended, on the death of the person in whom such property was vested, to vest in his executors and administrators, with sufficient distinctness to prevent questions of some doubt and difficulty from arising on this point. Real estate may be vested in a man in fee, in tail, or for life only; and it might have been expected that the section would either have been worded after the more elaborately framed model furnished by section 30 of the Conveyancing and Law of Property Act, 1881, with necessary modifications; or else, that it should have been expressed that the real estate should pass only to the extent of the estate or interest which was vested in the owner at his death.

Quantity of estate vesting in personal representatives.

Chap. III.

Observation on the wording of s. 1 (1).

What the sub-section says (omitting words not material to the present purpose), is, that real estate vested in any person without a right in any other person to take by survivorship, shall on his death vest in his personal representatives. No qualification is annexed to the expression "real estate," which expression *primâ facie* is open to the meaning that the whole real estate, *i.e.*, the fee simple in the property (whether the owner was seised of the real estate for an estate of inheritance or not), the whole fee would by virtue of the Act pass to his executors or administrators. This cannot possibly have been the intention, as, where real estate is limited to A. for life, with remainder to B., the result of vesting the fee in A.'s personal representatives on his death with powers of dealing with it, would be to take B.'s property away from him for the payment of A.'s debts. Such a construction is too manifestly absurd to be maintainable, and it must be taken that only estates of inheritance, viz., estates in fee and in tail, or only the former, are to be deemed to come within the operation of Part I. of the Act of 1897. It is now proposed to consider what estates and interests are presumably intended and will probably be held to be included in this sub-section.

As to estates vested in deceased owner in fee simple.

Estates of inheritance in realty may be limited in fee by such words as "to A. and his heirs," or "to A. for life, and after his death to his heirs" (*y*). The word "heirs," in either case, is a word of limitation, and the effect is to vest in A. himself the estate of inheritance, which he may freely alienate *inter vivos*, or devise by his will, so as to disappoint the heir, who accordingly takes, not as purchaser or by any right of survivorship, but takes, or would have taken but for the passing of this Act, as real representative of the deceased owner, only such real property as was not disposed of at his

---

(*y*) *Shelley's case,* 1 Rep. 94. See Jarman on Wills (5th ed.) Vol. II., pp. 1177, *et seq.*

death. Therefore, whether a man is seised in fee simple in possession, or by way of vested remainder, such estate of inheritance will at his death vest in his personal representatives. The question of contingent remainders will be considered later.

As to estates vested in fee tail.

The estate tail is also an estate of inheritance in the owner himself; so that the heir in tail does not take by right of survivorship, but takes under the limitation, and not as purchaser. This is so whether the estate tail is limited to a man and the heirs of his body generally, or to him and the heirs of his body by a particular wife (z). In the latter case, however, an estate in tail special is created, so that upon the death of the particular wife without issue of their two bodies living, the husband becomes tenant in tail after possibility of issue extinct, and has, in effect, nothing more than an estate for his life (a).

Devolution of estate tail.

It would therefore seem that the real estate of the deceased tenant in tail will on his death pass to his personal representatives to the full extent of the estate tail. If then, the estate of a deceased tenant in tail in possession vests in his personal representatives, on his death, such representatives will become and continue to be entitled to such estate, until they convey the same to the next heir in tail, who, but for the passing of this Act, would be entitled to the immediate possession of such estate. The result would be the same on the falling into possession during their tenure of an estate tail in remainder vested in a deceased owner. The representatives will therefore, during the period of administration, be entitled to receive the rents and profits and apply the same towards payment of the debts, etc., of a deceased tenant in tail. The

(z) The rule in *Shelley's case* applies no less to estates tail as to estates in fee simple. Co. Litt. 22 b; *Manderille's case*, Co. Litt. 26 b.

(a) *Williams* v. *Williams*, 12 East, 209.

effect of this enactment would thus seem to be to substitute temporarily the representatives for the heir in tail and to constitute them his involuntary assigns, holding a position in some respects analogous to that of a trustee in bankruptcy.

Devolution of base fee.

Similarly, if a person has died entitled to an estate tail in remainder, which has been barred in his lifetime without the consent of the protector of the settlement and so converted into a base fee, then that estate will pass to the extent of the base fee, so as to enable the personal representatives to deal with the reversionary estate so vested by way of sale or mortgage for the purpose of administration. But unless the consent of the protector of the settlement can be obtained, or unless he dies during the period of administration, the disentailing assurance cannot be perfected, nor can the land be conveyed by anyone to a purchaser or mortgagee so as to bar the persons entitled under the entail other than the direct issue of the tenant in tail.

Powers of sale, etc., under the Settled Land Acts.

Assuming the views above indicated to be correct, it would seem to follow that the executors or administrators of a deceased tenant in tail (other than tenant in tail after possibility of issue extinct), or a person entitled to a base fee, provided that the estate is in possession, or falls into possession during their tenure, will have the powers of sale and mortgage given to tenants for life by the Settled Land Acts (*b*), and will accordingly be able to sell and convey the fee in the settled land or any part thereof, or any easement, right, or privilege of any kind over or in relation to the same; and that they will also be able to mortgage the fee of the settled land or any part thereof for the purpose of discharging incumbrances thereon and other purposes mentioned in the Settled Land Acts.

(*b*) 45 & 46 Vict. c. 38, s. 18; 53 & 54 Vict. c. 69, s. 11.

But, if so, the moneys thus raised by sale or mortgage of settled land of which the last owner was tenant in tail, or for a base fee, will be capital money arising under these Acts (*c*), and accordingly the money must be paid not to the executors or administrators, but to the trustees of the settlement (*d*), and must be applied by the latter strictly in accordance with the provisions of the Acts (*e*), and, so far as not so applied, must " be held for and go to the same persons successively in the same manner and for and on the same estates, interests, and trusts as the land wherefrom the money arises would, if not disposed of, have been held and have gone under the settlement " (*f*). This being so, it is obvious that money raised by sale or mortgage of the settled lands cannot be applied by the executors or administrators of a deceased tenant in tail, or owner of a base fee, in payment of his debts, or other expenditure of or incident to the administration of his general estate.

Application of moneys raised by sales, etc., under the statutory powers.

In order, then, to render the corpus of settled land available for payment of debts, etc., of a deceased tenant in tail or owner of a base fee, it would be necessary for his executors or administrators to bar the entail or enlarge the base fee, as the case may require; otherwise, they will not be able to convey the fee simple to a purchaser or mortgagee so as to bind the persons entitled under the entail. The question is, have the executors or administrators power to do this?

Whether real representatives can bar an entail.

With the exception of certain estates tail granted by the Crown by way of reward for public services, and some such estates which have been created by particular Acts of Parliament, it has long been settled that the right to bar the entail is an essential and inseparable incident to an estate tail, and that any attempt to

Estates tail generally barrable.

(*c*) 45 & 46 Vict. c. 38, s. 2 (9).　　(*e*) *Ib.* s. 21.
(*d*) *Ib.* s. 22 (1).　　(*f*) *Ib.* s. 22 (5).

restrain this right is void (*g*). A doubt might, therefore, possibly suggest itself whether the executors or administrators of a deceased tenant in tail, as being themselves for the time being tenants in tail of the settled lands, might not at any time until they convey the estates to the person next in succession under the entail, bar the estate tail if in possession, or if it falls into possession during their tenure, or if in remainder, then with the consent of the protector of the settlement; and that, having so barred the entail, they might not be able to make a good title and convey the fee simple in the settled land free from the entail to a purchaser or a mortgagee.

It is, however, conceived that there are no sufficient grounds for such a contention. It must be borne in mind that the above observations only express the writer's views of the effect of the enactment under consideration as regards the vesting of "real estates" on the death of a tenant in tail; and, even if those views are correct, the statute does not give to the personal representatives any express power to bar the entail (*h*). It would be a curious and startling result of this Act, if, in the absence of any express provision, it were to be held that persons in possession of the land temporarily and for a limited purpose, have the power to alter the nature of the estate of an actual tenant in tail even for his presumable benefit, without his consent, and, perhaps, without his knowledge, or even against his wishes. Moreover, even if, as above suggested, the personal representatives of a deceased tenant in tail are to be regarded as the involuntary assigns of the person next entitled under the entail, yet they cannot, as such

---

(*g*) *Taltarum's case*, Year Book, 12 Edw. 4, 19; *Mary Partington's case*, 10 Rep. 36; see Co. Litt. 224 a; Fearne C. R. 260.

(*h*) By the Bankruptcy Act, 1883 (46 & 47 Vict. c. 52), s. 56 (5), trustees in bankruptcy are empowered to "deal with any property to which the bankrupt is beneficially entitled as tenant in tail in the same manner as the bankrupt might have dealt with it."

be in a better position than a purchaser for value or mortgagee, who, as is well known, has no power to bar the entail. In the absence of any statutory provisions specifically dealing with the point, all that can be done is to draw inferences from settled rules of law, and to endeavour to apply those rules to an entirely novel situation created by a statute which certainly does not err in the direction of prolixity or elaboration of detail. It may therefore be considered as clear that a purchaser or mortgagee cannot safely accept a title purporting to be made under a deed of disentailer or enlargement executed by the executors or administrators of a deceased tenant in tail or owner of a base fee, unless indeed the power of executors or administrators to make such a title should be affirmed by judicial decision.

Tenants in tail in possession of freeholds may generally, by means of a deed duly enrolled, sell and convey to a purchaser the fee simple in the lands completely discharged from the entail; and, of course, the lands being so discharged, the money representing the lands is also discharged in like manner as if the tenant in tail had first executed and enrolled a disentailing assurance of the land, and then conveyed it by a separate deed. Assuming, therefore, that contrary to the view above expressed, the executors or administrators are for the time being tenants in tail of the settled lands, each competent to bar the entail for the purpose of conveying the lands to a purchaser, it is conceived that the effect of a conveyance by them duly enrolled would have the effect of rendering the surplus moneys not required for purposes of administration the absolute property of the person who, but for the conveyance, would have been next entitled to the lands under the entail.

Destination of surplus sale or mortgage moneys.

On the same assumption, the case of a mortgage of the fee by the executors or administrators of a tenant in tail would seem to be governed by section 21 of the Fines and Recoveries Act (*i*), whereby a disposition under this Act by a tenant in tail, by way of mortgage of the fee, is to be "an absolute bar in equity as well as at law to all persons as against whom such disposition is by this Act authorized to be made;" the effect of which appears to be, that if the executors or administrators can and do make a valid mortgage in fee with a provision for redemption in the common form, they would thenceforth be owners in fee simple subject to the mortgage, and will be absolutely entitled to the surplus proceeds (if any), but would hold the lands and moneys as trustees for the person entitled thereto, being the person who, but for the mortgage, would be the next tenant in tail under the settlement.

As to obtaining concurrence of the next tenant in tail.

It is, however, conceived, notwithstanding the doubts above suggested, as to whether the executors or administrators of a deceased tenant in tail may not have power to make a good title to the fee on a sale or mortgage, that the power of barring the entail during the possession of the executors or administrators remains vested in the person who, but for this Act, would be entitled as next tenant in tail in possession. By the Fines and Recoveries Act (*k*), section 15, it is enacted "that every actual tenant in tail whether in possession, remainder, contingency, or otherwise, shall have full power to dispose of for an estate in fee simple absolute, or for any less estate, the lands entailed," as against all persons claiming in remainder under the settlement. And by section 22 of the same Act, it is enacted that "if at the time when there shall be a tenant in tail of lands under a settlement, there shall be subsisting in the same lands or any of them under the same settlement, any estate for years determinable on the dropping of a life or lives, or any greater estate, not being an estate for years prior to the estate

(*i*) 3 & 4 Will. 4, c. 74.
(*k*) 3 & 4 Will. 4, c. 74. As to the power to enlarge base fee see s. 39 of the same Act.

tail," then the owner of such prior estates, or of the first of such prior estates, if more than one, shall be the protector of the settlement; and by section 34, where there is a protector, his consent is made requisite to enable an "actual tenant in tail to create a larger estate than a base fee." If, therefore, the executors or administrators are to be regarded as owners of the prior estate "under the settlement," the next tenant in tail can effectually bar the entail with their consent; if they are not such owners, he can do so independently of their consent.

Chap. III.

Where a fee simple in real estate is settled upon several persons in succession, as, for instance, if it be limited to the use of A. for life, with remainder to B. in fee, then upon the death of A., B. does not take by right of survivorship, so as to come within the meaning of section 1, sub-section (1) of the Act of 1897, but by virtue of the settlement itself, under which he had a vested remainder during A.'s lifetime.

As to estates for life vested in a deceased person.

Although upon a strict construction the sub-section seems to say that the real estate, which was vested in A. during his life, is to vest by virtue of the Act in his personal representatives, so as to enable them to deal with the fee as they please under the Act for the purposes of administration, as has been already seen (*l*), yet this cannot possibly have been the intention of the Act. It may, therefore, be safely assumed that upon the death of a tenant for life under a settlement, the settled real estate will not come within the operation of the Act, but will pass immediately to the remainderman, as if the Act had not passed.

Estates *pur autre vie*, limited to the heir as special occupant, are specially mentioned in section 30 of the Conveyancing and Law of Property Act, 1881 (*m*), and

As to estates *pur autre vie*.

(*l*) See *ante*, p. 26.   (*m*) 44 & 45 Vict. c. 41.

are thereby, if vested on any trust or by way of mortgage, in any person solely, expressly made to pass to his personal representatives. The Act of 1897 does not mention such estates, and it seems open to doubt whether they pass on the death of the owner by virtue of the Act to his personal representatives, or whether they will not devolve immediately on the heir as heretofore. Estates *pur autre vie* limited to a man and his heirs, being freehold tenements, would seem to be "real estates," and so *primâ facie* to devolve by virtue of the Act of 1897 on personal representatives. But an estate *pur autre vie* so limited, though a tenement, is not a hereditament or estate of inheritance, and therefore not entailable within the statute De Donis (*n*), so that no common recovery would formerly have been suffered of it (*o*). Such estates have long been alienable *inter vivos* by the owner (*p*), and are devisable by his will (*q*), whereby his heir may be disappointed; but if not so disposed of, the estate (apart from this Act) will devolve on the heir not as such but as special occupant (*r*), that is to say, not by virtue of the words of limitation in the grant of the estate, nor as taking by way of representative a *quasi* fee simple vested in the deceased owner himself, but as a *persona designata* specifically described in the grant and taking by way of purchase. In other words, the grantee of an estate for life limited to him and his heirs, unless he disposes of the whole estate by deed or will as he has power to do, is virtually a mere tenant for life, and the heir takes as remainderman an independent interest. It may be said that the grantee had power to dispose of the whole estate in his lifetime or by his will if he had chosen to do so, and

---

(*n*) 13 Edw. 1. c. 1.
(*o*) *Grey* v. *Mannock*, 2 Eden. 339.
(*p*) Challis, R. P. 290.
(*q*) 1 Vict. c. 26, s. 3.
(*r*) *Ripley* v. *Waterworth*, 7 Ves. at p. 438. General occupancy is abolished by the statute, 29 Car. 2, c. 3, s. 12; and estates *pur autre vie*, where there is no special occupant, devolve and are applicable as personalty. See statute 14 Geo. 2. c. 20, s. 9.

that therefore the property which was so absolutely at his disposal ought to be made available to satisfy his creditors if required. It may be quite reasonable that this should be so, but the Legislature has not said so. The property not having been disposed of by the grantee, his interest therein is absolutely determined by his death, and the property has become the property of the heirs by way of remainder. The same reasoning, which goes to show that it cannot have been the meaning of the Act of 1887, that on the death of a tenant for life of settled lands the whole fee should vest in his personal representatives and be available for payment of his debts, seems to apply, though not so manifestly by way of *reductio ad absurdum*, to the case of an estate *pur autre vie* limited to the grantee and his heirs, and which the grantee has not disposed of. Anyhow, it will not do to blow hot and cold in construing the same enactment.

Estates *pur autre vie* coming into the hands of the heir by reason of a special occupancy are chargeable in his hands as assets by descent (*s*).

Estates *pur autre vie* are assets.

5. Appointment of Real Estates under General Powers.

Section 1 of the Act of 1897 further enacts that :—
(2.) This section shall apply to any real estate over which a person executes by will a general power of appointment as if it were real estate vested in him.

Application of s. 1 to appointments.

A general power as distinguished from a particular or limited power is thus defined by Lord *St. Leonards* (*t*): " By a general power we understand a right to appoint to whomsoever the donee pleases. By a

General and particular forms of appointment distinguished.

(*s*) 29 Car. 2, c. 3, s. 12.   (*t*) Sugd. Powers (8th ed.) 394.

particular power it is meant that the donee is restricted to some objects designated in the deed creating the power, as to his own children. A general power is, in regard to the estates which may be created by force of it, tantamount to a limitation in fee, not merely because it enables the donee to limit a *fee*, which a particular power may also do, but because it enables him to give the fee to whom he pleases; he has an absolute disposing power over the estate, and may bring it into the market whenever his necessities or wishes may lead him to do so."

<small>A general gift shall include estates over which the testator has a general power of appointment.</small>

By section 27 of the Wills Act (*u*) it is enacted that "a general devise of the real estate of the testator in any place or in the occupation of any person mentioned or otherwise described in a general manner, shall be construed to include any real estate or any real estate which such description shall extend, as the case may be, which he may have power to appoint in any manner he may think proper, and shall operate as an execution of such power unless a contrary intention shall appear by the will."

The rule in administration which has hitherto prevailed with regard to general powers of appointment is thus stated by Mr. *Farwell*(*v*):—" Both real and personal estate, subject to general powers of appointment, become assets for payment of the appointor's debts if the power is actually exercised in favour of volunteers; and it makes no difference whether the power is exerciseable by deed or by will, or by will only (*x*)."

<small>Effect of this enactment.</small>

The effect of the above sub-section therefore appears to be to give legislative confirmation to this rule as regards realty, actually appointed by will. But to render such realty assets in the hands of the real

---

(*u*) 1 Vict. c. 26.
(*v*) Farwell, Powers, 254.
(*x*) See *Jenney* v. *Andrews*, 6 Madd. 264; *Fleming* v. *Richardson*, 3 De. G. M. & G. 976; *Williams* v. *Lomas*, 16 Beav. 1.

representatives of the deceased instead of as heretofore in the hands of the appointee.

Chap. III.

In order, however, to render real estate over which a person has power to appoint, by will, assets in the hands of his real representatives, the power must have been actually executed, for equity will not aid the non-execution of a power (*y*).

Appointment must have been made.

Under the former law, although property appointed by will under a general power was assets for payment of debts, so that the claims of creditors prevailed over volunteers, yet the equity of a *bonâ fide* purchaser for value from a person taking under a voluntary deed of appointment was preferred to that of general creditors having no specific charge. This rule would appear still to prevail as regards personalty, but the present Act, by expressly enacting that real estate appointed by will, like real estate vested in the deceased person, shall pass to his personal representatives on his death, seems to deprive the appointee of any estate or interest in the property, so that he cannot make a good title to it or effectually convey it to a purchaser, until the personal representatives have assented to the appointment or conveyed the property to the appointee (*z*).

Appointee cannot make good title till assent.

---

6. What "Real Estate" will pass to Executors or Administrators.

With the exceptions above noticed, the Act of 1897 enacts that "real estate" of a deceased person shall vest in his personal representatives. But it is to be observed that the Act nowhere contains any definition of the term "real estate." It can only be presumed, though no doubt with some confidence, that the intention of the Act is to include and bring within its

No statutory definition given of "real estate."

(*y*) *Holmes* v. *Coghill*, 7 Ves. 499.
(*z*) *George* v. *Milbanke*, 9 Ves.
170; *Hart* v. *Middlehurst*, 3 Atk.
937; 3 Sugd. Powers 29 (6th ed.)

CHAP. III.

Ordinary meaning of "real estate."

operation all kinds of property which are generally recognized among lawyers as being real estate.

"Real estate" in the sense commonly accepted by lawyers is equivalent to "tenements," which latter expression includes not only "lands" in the narrower sense of that term, but also all rights of an incorporeal nature incident to or concerning land which have a substantive though invisible being, whether the estate of the owner devolves, or would, but for this Act devolve, on his heir or not (a). It is curious to observe that after section 1 the expression "real estate" is generally dropped, and the expression "land" frequently occurs, with presumably the same signification; that expression is defined to include "all hereditaments corporeal and incorporeal" (b).

Meaning of "land" in Acts of Parliament.

By the Interpretation Act, 1889 (c), in the construction of an Act of Parliament, unless the contrary intention appears, the expression "lands" is to include messuages, lands, tenements, and hereditaments, houses and buildings of any tenure. In the Act of 1897 sufficient indications of contrary intention appear to exclude from its operation copyholds, customary freeholds, and leaseholds, and to confine its application to freehold "lands" as thus defined.

The term "hereditaments" is of very wide significacation, and includes all real estate, corporeal and incorporeal, which on the death of the owner intestate would, on the common law, devolve on his heir (d).

Meaning of "real estate" in Act of 1897.

It may therefore be inferred that the Act of 1897 vests in the real representatives of a deceased owner all his "real estate" or "land" whatsoever, with the exception of copyholds, customary freeholds and leaseholds, including not only his land in the

---

(a) Co. Litt. 4a, 19b, 20a; see R. v. *Tolpuddle* (*Inhabitants of*), 4 T. R. 671; see also Burton's Compendium, 1, 3.

(b) See s. 24 of the Act.
(c) 52 & 53 Vict. c. 53, s. 3.
(d) Co. Litt. 6a; Shep. Touchst. 91.

common acceptation of the term, with all houses, buildings, timber, and growing produce erected or being thereon, and mines thereunder (e), but also all his real property of an incorporeal nature such as manors, advowsons, tithes, easements, profits *à prendre*, rent charges, and fee farm and other rents and franchises and offices annexed to lands, and other rights.

As regards land in the narrowest sense of the word, with the houses, etc., thereon, the result of the Act may in some cases be to cause considerable and somewhat unpleasant surprise in the minds of devisees and expectant heirs, and other persons. The widow or eldest son of a deceased owner in fee will find themselves liable, certainly for a year from the death, and perhaps for a much longer period, to be excluded from the marital or paternal home; and if they do remain in occupation of the same, it will only be by the permission or acquiescence of the real representatives, who would have it in their power, and indeed would be bound, so long as there is any risk of the personalty proving insufficient for payment of the debts of the deceased, or any legacies given by his will or any codicil thereto, to charge the devisee or heir with a rent in respect of such occupation, and to accumulate such rent to meet the contingent risk. This enactment may also in some cases operate so as to interrupt the continuity of the management of the estate; as for instance, if a father has carried on a freehold farm with the assistance of his eldest son, to whom he devises the farm, but does not appoint him executor. On the father's death, the son will be liable to be excluded from all control and management of the farm, unless the executors, as real representatives of the father, see fit to employ him as manager; and he would also be liable to be charged an occupation rent for the farm during the period of

Some effects of the vesting of "lands" in executors or administrators.

(e) Co. Litt. 4a, b, Shep. Touchst. 92; 2 Black. Com. 218.

administration, or to hand over the net rents and profits to the real representatives, though probably as against such payments, wholly or in part, he would be entitled to set off a claim for his salary as manager.

Such cases will, however, probably not be of frequent occurrence. Leaving out for the present the question of settled lands, which will be hereafter considered, testators who are owners of real estates of inheritance will probably be careful to appoint the devisee of such estates as one of the executors, and in cases of intestacy it may be expected that the heir-at-law will be appointed by the court to be administrator of the real estate of the deceased, and so that he will be entitled solely or jointly with others to the possession and control of the property. Or it may happen that the real representatives may without risk to themselves let the devisee or heir-at-law into possession shortly after the owner's death, either because there is no reasonable prospect of the real estate being required in due course of administration for payment of debts, etc., or because a sufficient sum to meet the liabilities has been raised by mortgage or sale of part of the land.

Incorporeal hereditaments vest in executors or administrators.

It has been seen above that the expression "land" in Acts of Parliament generally, and in the Act of 1897 includes incorporeal hereditaments, which will accordingly by virtue of this Act vest in the executors or administrators of a deceased person in whom such hereditaments were vested at his death.

Manors and manorial rights.

Copyholds are holden of a manor and are parcels thereof. A manor is constituted by the union, by virtue of an ancient grant of the Crown, of the freehold estate in the lands (commonly called the demesnes) of the manor, with the seignory over all lands within the manor (*f*).

(*f*) Co. Cop. s. 31.

The seignory includes the freehold estate in all copyholds, parcels of the manor, waste lands within the manor, generally the right to mines, minerals, and timber; the right to hold courts; to grant licences to copyholders to lease their lands; to demand heriots on deaths of tenants; to demand fines on admittances, rents, suits and services according to the custom of the manor; to enforce forfeiture on alienation and other acts contrary to the customary tenure; and last, but not least, the right of escheat, whereby on the death of a tenant in customary fee simple without leaving a customary heir, and without having incurred forfeiture to the Crown, as by treason (*g*), the lord may enter on and recover possession of the land. The lord so entering is not strictly a purchaser, but the land acquired by escheat is united to and devolves with the seignory to which the right of entry is attached (*h*).

Chap. III. Incidents of a seignory.

A seignory also includes the true freehold of what are usually termed "customary freeholds," but their essential characteristics are the same as those of copyholds, inasmuch as the existence, nature and incidents of the tenure depend on custom and not on the common law, and admittance by the lord is necessary to complete the title of the tenant whether he takes by devise, descent, or purchase for value (*i*). The rents and services issuing out of such lands will pass by grant of a manor (*j*).

Customary freeholds.

A manor being an incorporeal hereditament of a freehold nature, will devolve, on the death of the lord on or after January 1st, 1898, on his executors or administrators, who will be the proper persons to demand and recover heriots, fines, and rents, to hold

Devolution of manors on executors or administrators.

(*g*) Forfeiture for treason, etc., is now abolished.
(*h*) Co. Litt. 18 b, Hargreaves' note.
(*i*) Burton's Compendium, 1283; Challis on Real Property, 26; see *Doe* v. *Huntington*, 4 East, 271.
(*j*) Co. Litt. 58 a; Bl. Comm. 53.

courts, to grant licences to tenants of the manor to lease their lands, and to exercise and enforce all other manorial rights, powers, and privileges.

Advowsons.

An advowson or right of presentation to an ecclesiastical benefice is also an incorporeal hereditament, and therefore " real estate " within the meaning of the Act of 1897, and will vest accordingly in the executors or administrators of a deceased patron, who may sell or mortgage it for the purposes of administration.

Right of nomination to benefice during period of administration.

It is clear that the legal right of presentation resides during the period of administration in these representatives as owners of the advowson, but it does not seem clear in whom the right to nominate is vested in case of a vacancy occurring during that period. Should this question require judicial determination it will be one of first impression, and can only be decided upon reasonings from analogy or general principles.

Analogies of rules as to mortgages and bankruptcy.

The two classes of cases which alone appear to furnish analogies available for this purpose are those of mortgagees and of trustees in bankruptcy.

Mortgagor's right to nominate.

Where an advowson is in mortgage, the right to present is at law in the mortgagee as having the legal estate (*k*); but he is in equity compelled to present the nominee of the mortgagor, for the mortgagee can make no profit by presenting to the church to sink or lessen his debt, and the mortgagee therefore in that case until the foreclosure is but in the nature of a trustee for the mortgagor (*l*). By the Act of 1897 (*m*) it is expressly enacted that the real representative is to be a trustee for the person beneficially entitled, and it would therefore seem that the analogy of the case of a mortgagee is pertinent, and that on the same principle a real representative may be held to be compellable to present the nominee of the devisee or heir.

(*k*) *Dyer* v. *Craven*, 2 Dick. 662.
(*l*) *Jory* v. *Cox*, Prei. Ch. 71.
(*m*) See s. 2, sub-s. (1), *post*, p. 52.

The analogy of the relations between a trustee in bankruptcy and the debtor appears to be even closer for the purposes of this question than those between mortgagor and mortgagee, inasmuch as a trustee in bankruptcy is trustee first for the creditors, and, subject to the satisfaction of their claims, for the debtor. It has long been settled under the former bankruptcy law that if a bankrupt was the patron of an advowson, it would pass to his assignees who might sell it at any time, except when vacant, in the ordinary way, but that if a vacancy occurred before the advowson was sold, the bankrupt, and not the assignee, should present, because the void turn of a church is not valuable (n). This rule has since been affirmed by statute (o).

Chap. III.
Bankrupt's right to nominate.

Bearing in mind that the main object of Part I. of the Act of 1897 appears to vest the real estate as well as the personal estate of a deceased person in his representatives for the purpose of more convenient realization of administration, that the representatives are not to remain in possession longer than is necessary for such purpose, and that while they are in possession, they are apparently trustees for the devisee or heir, and so bound to consider his interests, and that a vacant benefice is unsaleable, and therefore of no material value in increasing the assets for payment of debts, etc., it is on general principles submitted that the right of nomination to a vacancy occurring during the period of administration will be in the devisee or heir and not in the real representatives.

Consideration of the question on general principles.

On the other hand, it must be remembered that the allowance to executors of a right to nominate and present to a vacant benefice any person whom they may select, is not unknown to the law. If one be seised of

Right of executors to present their own nominee in certain cases.

(n) Burns, Eccl. Law, Vol. I., tit. Benefice (I., 4); see *Exp.*   *Maymont*, 1 Atk. 196.
(o) 12 & 13 Vict. c. 106, s. 147.

Chap. III.   an advowson in fee, and the church doth become void, the void turn is a chattel; and if the patron dieth before he doth present, the avoidance doth not go to his heir, but to his executors; and if the testator do present, and (his clerk not being admitted) then his executors do present their clerk, the ordinary is at his election which clerk he will receive (*p*). But hitherto, where the vacancy has been occasioned by the death of a patron, he being incumbent, the right of the heir or devisee to present his own nominee has prevailed (*q*).

Tithes.   Tithes are incorporeal hereditaments of ecclesiastical origin, which at common law could not be held by a layman (*r*), but which by virtue of the confiscating statutes of Henry VIII. have in many instances ceased to be the property of the church (*s*). Tithes in the hands of lay impropriators are included in the expression "tenements" in its wider sense (*t*), and are expressly made "hereditaments" by statute (*u*), accordingly come within the definition of "land" in the Interpretation Act, 1889 (*x*), and consequently within the operation of the Act of 1897, so as to devolve on the executor or administrator of a tithe owner dying on or after January 1st, 1897 (*y*).

Rent-charges.   Rent-charges and other freehold rents are also incorporeal hereditaments, and will pass by virtue of the Act of 1897, in cases to which that Act applies, on the death of a person entitled thereto, for an estate of inheritance, to his executors or administrators as "real estate." If a man seised of lands grant a yearly rent,

---

(*p*) Watson, Eccl. Law, c. 9; Burn, Eccl. Law, Vol. I., tit. Benefice (3, 5).
(*q*) *Holt* v. *Winchester*, 3 Sw. 47; see 7 B. & Cr. 147.
(*r*) *Sherwood* v. *Winchcombe*. Cro. Eliz. 293.
(*s*) 27 Hen. 8, c. 28; 31 Hen. 8, c. 13; and see as to Ireland, 32 & 33 Vict. c. 42.

(*t*) *R.* v. *Shingle*, 1 Stra. 100; *R.* v. *Ellis*, 3 Cri. 323.
(*u*) 32 Hen. 8, c. 7.
(*x*) *Ante*, p. 38.
(*y*) Tithes have been very generally commuted for statutory rent-charges under several Acts of Parliament which need not be here referred to.

to be issuing out of the land, to another in fee or in tail, or for term of life, with a clause of distress, then it is a rent-charge; but if the grant be without a clause of distress, it is a rent seck, or a dry rent, to which at common law no distress was incident (z).

It is not uncommon, especially in the north of England, for land to be conveyed in fee, with a reservation to the grantor and his heirs of a perpetual rent-charge issuing thereout, commonly called a fee-farm rent. Formerly express powers of distress and entry were usually inserted in deeds of grant of rent-charges, but now their insertion is rendered unnecessary by the Conveyancing and Law of Property Act, 1881 (a), which enables the grantee of a rent-charge under instruments coming into operation after December 31st, 1881, to exercise such powers, though not expressly given by the instruments of grant, and also, if thought advisable, to limit a term of years to secure the rent-charge. These statutory powers being given "to the person entitled to receive the annual sum," will under the Act of 1897 be exerciseable by the executors or administrators of a grantor dying on or after January 1st, 1898, as being the persons so entitled during the period of administration.

Like rent-charges, New River shares (b) and River Avon shares (c) are real estate, and accordingly such shares, or fractional parts thereof, will devolve, under the Act of 1897, upon the personal representatives of a deceased owner.

In the ordinary acceptation of the term "real estate" also includes easements, which are incorporeal

---

(z) Co. Litt. 144a; Gilbert, Rents, 38; Hoy's Maxims, 132. The statute 4 Geo. 2, c. 28, s. 5, extended powers of distress to rents seck.

(a) 44 & 45 Vict. c. 41, s. 44.
(b) *Drybutter* v. *Bartholomew*, 2 P. Wms. 127.
(c) *Buckeridge* v. *Ingram*, 2 Ves. Sen. 652.

CHAP. III.
hereditaments (*d*). Easements have been thus defined: "An easement is a privilege, without profit, which the owner of one tenement has a right to enjoy in respect of that tenement, in or over the tenement of another person, by reason whereof the latter is obliged to suffer, or refrain from doing, something on his own tenement for the benefit of the former (*e*).

Profits *à prendre*.

Profits *à prendre* are also incorporeal hereditaments, and therefore "real estate," so as to pass, by virtue of the Act of 1897, to the personal representatives of a deceased person entitled thereto for an estate of inheritance. Profits *à prendre* differ from easements in that the former give to the grantee a right to appropriate or participate in the profits of land (*f*). The term includes rights of fowling or fishing (*g*), rights to enter on land of another for the purpose of felling trees (*h*), or of getting stones, gravel, or sand (*i*), and rights to pasture cattle on the lands of another (*k*).

The rights of shooting over the covers, moors, or fields, or fishing the streams or lakes of an estate will, by virtue of this Act, be taken away from the devisee or heirs, and vested in the executors or administrators until they assent to the devise or execute a conveyance of the rights to the devisee or heirs.

Titles of honour.

Titles of honour or dignities having been originally annexed to land (*l*), are considered as real estate, and are incorporeal hereditaments wherein persons may have a freehold. A peerage or baronetcy, however, is not alienable by the holder of the title during his

(*d*) *Hewlins* v. *Shippam*, 5 B. & Cr., at p. 229.
(*e*) Goddard on Easements, 2.
(*f*) Gale on Easements, 1, 8.
(*g*) *Pears* v. *Lacy*, 4 Mod. 355; see *Hooper* v. *Clark*, L. R. 2 Q. B. 200; *Webber* v. *Lee*, 9 Q. B. D. 315.

(*h*) *Bailey* v. *Stevens*, 12 C. B. (N.S.) 91.
(*i*) *Constable* v. *Nicholson*, 14 C. B. (N.S.) 230.
(*k*) *Bailey* v. *Appleyard*, 8 A. & E. 161.
(*l*) 1 Inst. 20a. See *Gerrard* v. *Gerrard*, 5 Mod. 64.

lifetime, nor disposable by his will, but on his death devolves upon his heir-male or heir general upon the terms of the patent, not like lands limited to a person in fee simple or in tail at the present day, by virtue of the estate of inheritance vested in that person (which estate would enable him to disappoint his heir by disposing of the same), but by right vested in the next lineal or collateral successor to the title. It is obvious, therefore, that titles of honour are within the exception to the operation of the statute now under consideration; not only on the general ground that such real estates are unsaleable and incapable of increasing the assets in the hands of personal representatives for the purposes of administration, but also because they are vested in the holders thereof with a right vested in their successors to take by survivorship, which accrues immediately upon the death of a former holder.

Another class of rights which would in strictness appear not to fall within the operation of the Act of 1897, are rights of entry for conditions broken, and other rights of entry on land. These rights are not within the exception on the ground of right of survivorship, nor are they otherwise expressly excepted from the operation of the Act of 1897. But section 1 of the Act of 1897, being an enactment which takes a certain species of property away from the person who is entitled thereto by the common law, and gives that property to other persons, ought, on the recognized principles of construction of such enactments, to be strictly construed so as not to be held to extend to anything which is not expressly, or by necessary implication, included in the enactment. The property which this Act takes away from the devisee or heir, and gives to the personal representatives of a deceased person, is "real estate"; another Act, as has been seen, contains the definition of this expression for the purposes of the Act.

Rights of entry.

Rights of entry are generally created by express provisions in deeds of grant or demise of lands, whereby upon breach of covenants by the grantee or lessee or those claiming under him, or upon the happening of some other specified event, power is given to the grantor or lessor, "his heirs and assigns," to enter in and upon the premises granted or demised, and to repossess and enjoy the same as for his and their former estate. Such rights are not real estate; they confer no seisin nor any possessory interest in the land until actual entry; they were not formerly devisable by will, but descended according to the terms of the power upon the heir, so that the land and the right to sue for breach of covenants might devolve upon a devisee, but he might be unable to enforce the particular remedy given by the power without the concurrence of the heir. By the Wills Act (*m*), "All rights of entry for conditions broken and other rights of entry," were rendered devisable, but this enactment did not render such rights real estate in other respects.

According to the usual practice, however, powers of entry are expressly given not only to the donee and his heirs, but also to his assigns; and it may apparently be contended with some reason that, by virtue of the Act of 1897, the personal representatives of a deceased person are the involuntary assigns of his devisee or heir like the trustee in bankruptcy of a debtor (*n*). If this view is correct, then it would seem that a power of entry, if properly drawn so as to extend to assigns, will be exerciseable by the personal representatives of a deceased donee of the power as being his assigns.

(*m*) 1 Vict. c. 26, s. 3.   (*n*) See as to this, *post*, pp. 53, *et seq.*

7. As to Shifting Uses, Executory Devises, and Contingent Remainders.

Whether shifting uses, etc., are within the operation of Part I. of the Act of 1897.

Section 1, sub-section (1) of the Act of 1897 by enacting that real estate " vested " in a deceased person shall on his death vest in his personal representatives, seems to exclude from the operation of Part I. of the Act all real estate which was not vested in the deceased person at his death either in possession or remainder. If this is so, it follows that property to which a person was entitled under a shifting use or executory devise will, in some cases, be excluded, and the same will always happen where he was entitled by way of contingent remainder.

As to shifting uses.

Shifting or springing uses are created by deed, and are executory interests operating under the Statute of Uses (*o*). A conveyance to a person in fee to hold from a future date, or upon the happening of a given event, is void (*p*); but the desired result may be obtained by means of a shifting use. Thus a conveyance to A. to the use of the grantor and his heirs until January 1st, 1898, and thereafter to the use of B. and his heirs, is good; so also is a conveyance to A. to the use of the grantor and his heirs until he shall go to Rome (to use an illustration taken from old text books), and thereafter to the use of B. and his heirs. Now supposing B. to die before January 1st, 1898, or before the grantor goes to Rome, the result would seem to be different in the two cases. In the former case B. at his death has an estate in fee which must come into possession on the arrival of the specified date, *i.e.*, a vested interest, which will accordingly pass to his personal representatives by virtue of the Act. But in the second case, the happening of the event is uncertain, so that at the death of B. the real estate is not " vested " in him so as to pass

---

(*o*) 27 Hen. 8, c. 10.   (*p*) Blackst. Comm. 166.

to his personal representatives, unless a strained and unnatural construction is put on the word "vested," which construction can only be arrived at by guessing at what may be supposed to be the intention of the Act, though not expressed by its language if used in its accepted sense.

As to executory devises.

Executory devises are future estates or interest in land created by will which cannot consistently with the rules of law take effect as remainders (*q*). The following are instances of executory devises:— Devise in fee to A. and his heirs, to take effect at a given period after the testator's death; or devise to A. and his heirs if he shall return from Rome. Until the arrival of the date or the happening of the event, the fee simple has hitherto descended to the heir-at-law of the testator, and will under the recent Act descend to his personal representatives, but on the death of A. in the meantime it would seem that in the former case his estate or interest will, and in the latter case will not, pass under the Act to the personal representatives of A.

As to contingent remainders.

Contingent remainders differ from executory devises in that the latter interests are not in general liable to be affected by any alteration in the preceding estate; but contingent remainders must take effect, if at all, immediately upon the determination of the preceding estate of freehold, and if not ready to take effect they will fail altogether (*r*). The old rule was that no devise capable, according to the state of the objects at the death of the testator, of taking effect as a remainder, should be construed as to be an executory devise; but this rule has been altered by statute as regards wills executed after August 2nd, 1877 (*s*), whereby a contingent remainder which could have been valid as springing or shifting uses or executory devise without

---

(*q*) Jarman on Wills (5th ed.) Vol I., p. 822.

(*r*) *Ibid.*, p. 831.
(*s*) 40 & 41 Vict. c. 33.

a sufficient estate to support it, is made capable of taking effect as such notwithstanding failure of the particular estate before the remainder vests.

But contingent remainders, which are only capable of taking effect as such, may be and often are created. Thus land may be given by deed or will to A. and his heirs unless and until he shall go to Rome, but, if he shall go there, then to B. and his heirs; if A. goes to Rome in B.'s lifetime, B.'s estate in fee becomes vested in possession, and on his death will vest in his personal representatives under the Act ; if A. dies without having gone to Rome in B.'s lifetime, A.'s estate in fee will have become absolute, and will vest in his personal representatives to the exclusion of B.; but if B. dies in A.'s lifetime there is no certainty that A. will not go to Rome, so that at B.'s death he has no "vested" interest (in the ordinarily accepted sense of the term) which can pass to his personal representatives, so that even if A. does go to Rome during the period of administration, the interest then falling into possession would apparently escape the operation of Part I. of the Act, and devolve on the devisee or heir-at-law of A.

Conditions depending on events the happening of which is uncertain, attached to gifts by deed or will, are so generally personal, and, if not so, are so often such as to render the estate or interest given of little or no marketable value for the purpose of raising money for administration until the event happens or cannot happen, that it is quite possible that the Legislature may have designedly intended to exclude gifts to which conditions are attached as not worth consideration.

CHAPTER IV.

OF THE NATURE AND EXTENT OF THE INTEREST IN REAL ESTATE TAKEN BY EXECUTORS AND ADMINISTRATORS.

1. Nature of the Interest.

The Act of 1897 contains the following enactment:—

Provisions as to administration.

Section 2.—(1.) Subject to the powers, rights, duties, and liabilities herein-after mentioned, the personal representatives of a deceased person shall hold the real estate as trustees for the persons by law beneficially entitled thereto, and those persons shall have the same power of requiring a transfer of real estate as persons beneficially entitled to personal estate have of requiring a transfer of such personal estate.

By section 24, sub-section (2) of this Act the expression "personal representatives" means an executor or administrator.

Effect of this sub-section.

The effect of this and the four following sub-sections of section 2 is to constitute the personal representatives of a deceased person owners of his real estate for purposes of administration, and to arm them with powers over that estate similar to those which they now have over the personalty, for such purposes, and to impose upon them corresponding liabilities for acts done or omitted in the course of administration.

Liability of the interest of executors and administrators in real estate considered.

With regard to personal estate, it has been laid down that the interest which an executor or administrator has in the goods of the deceased person is very different from the absolute, proper and ordinary interest which everyone has in his own proper goods (*t*); for an executor or administrator has his estate as such in another right merely, viz., as the minister or dispenser of the goods of the dead (*u*). What, however, is the precise nature of this "other right" in virtue of which an executor or administrator holds the property of the deceased, does not seem to be precisely defined.

The estate or interest taken by the executors or administrators of a deceased owner of real estate must apparently be in its quality one of two things: it must be regarded either as an artificial prolongation of the deceased person's life until the termination of the period of administration, or as a new estate or interest involuntary by way of assignment, during that period, of the estate or interest of the devisee or heir, or heir of the body of the deceased owner, but paramount to such last-mentioned estate or interest.

The first of these alternative views would no doubt afford a ready and easy solution to doubts and difficulties (which have been noticed in the preceding chapter) with regard to the devolution upon executors or administrators of estates tail, estates *pur autre vie*, and other matters. Executors or administrators are generally called *personal* representatives, not because the personal estate vests in them, but because they *represent* the *person* of the testator or intestate; and it might be urged, perhaps with some show of reason, that they thus are in legal effect, the deceased owner himself, and hold whatever estate or interest he held, at his actual death, and may accordingly exercise all powers of dealing with the estate, which he could have exercised if he was alive, and had constituted himself trustee from the date of his actual death for the persons

Whether such interest is that of the deceased owner or a new interest.

(*t*) Wentw. Off. Ex. 192; see Williams on Executors (9th ed.), Vol. I., p. 558.

(*u*) *Pinchon's case*, 9 Rep. 38b. See 2 Inst. 236.

next entitled to the property. Thus, if he was entitled in fee, they could deal with the property as they might think fit, having regard nevertheless to their duties as trustees; if he had an estate in tail, they would have power to bar the entail with or without the consent of the protector of the settlement, as the case might be; and if he had an estate *pur autre vie*, they could disappoint the special occupant by alienation. But it would also consistently follow, according to this view, that, if the deceased person had only an estate for life, under a settlement or will, such estate must be deemed to continue after the date of his actual death until the estate has been fully administered, or until a surrender of the estate and interest of the dead man by the executors or administrators to the remainderman. The difficulty which militates against adopting this view is, that the whole scheme of the Act seems to be to put executors and administrators in the same position as regards realty as they have hitherto held as regards chattels real; and it has never been yet suggested that the estate and interest of executors or administrators in chattels real or other personalty is an artificial prolongation of the life of the testator or intestate, so as to entitle them to claim the rents and profits (other than emblements) of chattels real or the income of other personalty accruing after the date of the actual death of a person who has only a life interest in the property.

But further, not only does the Act of 1897 contain no provisions expressly or impliedly affirming an artificial prolongation of the life of a deceased owner of land, but any such implication is, as it is submitted, contrary to the language of the Act. Section 1, sub-section (1) of the Act expressly enacts that real estate vested in a deceased owner shall "vest" in his personal representatives; and this expression seems clearly to indicate the creation of a new estate devolving on them at the death.

Moreover, section 2, sub-section (2) of the Act, by referentially conferring on personal representatives powers of dealing with real estate, seems impliedly to negative the view that they possess all the powers of the owner by virtue of the prolongation of his life. The present writer has therefore adopted the view that the personal representatives of the deceased owner take an estate or interest in the realty paramount to or overriding the estate of the person or persons entitled as devisee or devisees, joint or successive, if more than one, or the person entitled as heir under an intestacy, or as heir of the body under a prior entail, but so that the quantity and incidents of such estates attach to the estate of the executors or administrators, thereby, in effect, constituting them the involuntary assigns of the person or persons so entitled for whom they are trustees,

That the estate of executors or administrators in the realty of a deceased person must be paramount to and override the estate of the persons who, subject thereto, are entitled to the property, is obvious both on the analogy of the estate taken by executors and administrators in chattels real, and also because such paramount estate with ancillary powers of selling or otherwise dealing with the property so as to override the estate of the devisee on him is absolutely necessary for the performance of their duties and the effectual carrying out of the administration; and this must be the case whether the whole fee passes by the will to a single devisee or several devisees jointly or successively, or under an intestacy to a single heir or to several heirs as co-parceners or under the custom of Gavelkind.

Where, however, a will devises land, even by way of legal limitations in strict settlement, to a person for life or to several persons consecutively for their lives, with remainders over, a question might arise whether

Chap. IV.

Question where there is a devise to a person for life with remainders over.

the effect of the Act of 1897 may not be, during the period of possession by the personal representatives of the testator, to create a state of things analogous to that which would have existed, if the devise had been to the personal representatives upon trusts corresponding to the uses above referred to; or, in other words, whether the devisees for life under the first use limited will be in the position of an equitable tenant for life, and thus be entitled to exercise the powers of sale, mortgaging, leasing, and accepting surrenders of leases, etc., given to limited owners by the Settled Land Acts (*x*).

Whether devisee for life can exercise power of sale, etc., under Settled Land Acts.

In favour of this view it might be urged that, though a tenant for life, whether legal or equitable, cannot exercise these statutory powers unless his estate is immediate and not in remainder or expectancy (*y*), yet that his possession need not be personal, and that the possession of trustees will not preclude him from exercising the powers, when he is entitled to the net rents and profits (*z*); and it might be further urged that in the case supposed, the devisee is entitled to the rents and profits not required for purposes of the administration of the testator's estate, if not during the continuance of the period of possession by the real representatives, at all events on the determination of the period (*a*). It must also be borne in mind that, even if the statute constitutes the personal representatives, in such a case, the involuntary assigns of the fee of the first taker, namely, the tenant for life under the will, the powers of selling, leasing, etc., under the Settled Land Acts remain exerciseable by a tenant for life, notwithstanding any assignment " by operation of law or otherwise " of his estate or interest (*b*).

(*x*) See 45 & 46 Vict. c. 38, s. 2, sub-ss. (5) and (10) (i).
(*y*) *Re Jones*, 26 Ch. D. 741; see *Re Clitheroe*, 31 Ch. D. 135 C. A.
(*z*) *Re Morgan*, 24 Ch. D. 114.
(*a*) See *post*, p. 58.
(*b*) 45 & 46 Vict. c. 38, s. 50.

Assuming that the correct view of the effect of the statute is to render the powers given by the Settled Land Acts exerciseable during the period of possession of the real representatives, it would seem to follow that such powers may be exercised by them on behalf of an infant, whether he is beneficially entitled in fee or for life, under a devise or intestacy. By the Settled Land Act, 1882 (c), section 50, an infant absolutely entitled to land is to be tenant for life thereof; and by section 60 of the same Act, the statutory powers of a tenant for life may apparently be exercised on his behalf by the trustees of the settlement, who would apparently be the personal representatives of the deceased owner as being "trustees" (d), and having a power of sale (e), and so being "trustees of the settlement" within the meaning of the Settled Land Acts (f).

Where an infant is entitled under a will or intestacy.

It is to be regretted that the Act of 1897 did not specifically define the nature of the estate to be taken by executors or administrators in realty, and, in particular, that it did not expressly lay down whether or not all or any of the powers of tenants for life under a will are to be suspended during the period of administration, and, if not, by whom such powers are to be exercised during that period. The omission may be productive of serious inconvenience in the case of large estates where the complication of the testator's affairs lead to a prolongation of the period; this may be especially so as regards granting leases of settled lands, as the powers of executors and administrators to lease for long terms of years is not free from doubt, as will be seen hereafter (g). On the whole, however, it is submitted that the operation of a devise, whether in fee or by way of settlement, is entirely postponed during the period of administration, and overridden by the

(c) 45 & 46 Vict. c. 38.
(d) See *ante*, p. 52.
(e) See *ante*, pp. 60, 69.
(f.) 45 & 46 Vict. c. 38, s. 2, sub-s. (8).
(g) *Post*, p. 75.

paramount estate of the executors, and by their powers incident thereto; and, accordingly, that, in the case of a settlement of lands created by will, the statutory powers of tenants for life under such settlement are suspended and incapable of exercise by anybody until the executors assent to the devise.

It is conceived that this must be so as regards the powers of a tenant for life to sell or mortgage the settled land, as otherwise there would be a conflict of powers which would seriously impede the executors in so dealing with the property for purposes of administration, and all the statutory powers of a tenant for life must stand or fall together.

As to estates tail.

The reasons have been already stated (*h*) for considering that an estate tail or base fee vested in a deceased person goes, under the Act of 1897, to his executors or administrators, but that they have no power to bar the entail or perfect a disentailing assurance so as to enable them to sell or otherwise deal with the fee simple discharged from the entail.

Executors and administrators are trustees.

The first clause of section 2, sub-section (1) of the Act of 1897, apparently renders the personal representatives trustees of the real estate throughout the period of administration, and not merely after they have fully administered. It thus seems to affirm and apply to real estate the rule hitherto recognized as to the position of executors and administrators with regard to personalty of which they become possessed as such; namely, that a Court of Equity considers the executors and administrators as trustees (*i*), and will compel them in the due execution of their trust to apply the property to the payment of debts and legacies, if any, and the surplus capital and income according to the will, or, in case of

---

(*h*) *Ante*, pp. 27 *et seq.*
(*i*) Williams on Executors, 9 ed., Vol. 1, p. 243. See *Farr* v.

Newman, 4 T. R. 621, 645, 2 R. R. 479.

intestacy, according to the Statute of Distributions (*k*); and, accordingly, an executor will be personally liable for all breaches of the ordinary trusts which in Courts of Equity are considered to arise from his office (*l*).

An administrator, after he has obtained a grant of administration, has an interest in the property of the deceased equal to that of an executor (*m*).

Interest of administrator equal to that of executor.

2. Duration of the Interest in Realty taken by Personal Representatives.

The concluding clause of section 2, sub-section (1) of the Act of 1897, must be taken together with the provisions contained in section 3, sub-section (2) of the same Act, which in effect enacts that, on the expiration of one year after the death of a deceased owner of real estate, the person next entitled thereto under the will or intestacy may apply to the court to compel a conveyance by the executors or administrators to him, a year being granted to them as the normal period of administration (*n*).

It will thus seem clear that the quantity of the estate and interest of the executors or administrators in realty is, by virtue of the Act, strictly limited by reference to their duties of and incident to the administration of the general estate, and that the duration of such estate or interest is also limited to the period necessary for the completion of such administration, or to such period as shall be required for ascertaining that the real estate will not be required in aid of the personalty for the purposes of the administration.

(*k*) Williams on Executors, (9th ed.) Vol. II. p. 1876. See *Adair* v. *Shaw*, 1 Sch. & L. 262. As to the rights of the heir on intestacy to realty not required for administration, see *post*, p. 84.

(*l*) *Re Marsden*, 26 Ch. D. 783, 789.
(*m*) Touchst., 474; *Blackborough* v. *Davis*, 1 P. Wms. 43.
(*n*) See *post*, p. 110.

CHAPTER V.

OF THE POWERS OF EXECUTORS AND ADMINISTRATORS IN RELATION TO REAL ESTATE.

1. GENERAL ENACTMENT AS TO POWERS, ETC., OF PERSONAL REPRESENTATIVES.

THE Act of 1897 contains no provisions specifically defining the powers, rights, duties of real representatives during or on the determination of the period of administration, but it merely applies to real estate by reference all the existing statute and case law with regard to personal estate generally, and chattels real in particular so far as applicable to real estate, with an exception which will be noticed in due course.

By section 2 of the Act it is enacted as follows :—

Referential application of rules of law as to chattels real to real estate.

(2.) All enactments and rules of law relating to the effect of probate or letters of administration as respects chattels real, and as respects the dealing with chattels real before probate or administration, and as respects the payment of costs of administration and other matters in relation to the administration of personal estate, and the powers, rights, duties and liabilities of personal representatives in respect of personal estate, shall apply to real estate so far as the same are applicable, as if that real estate were a chattel real vesting in them or him, save that it shall not be lawful for some or one only of several joint personal representatives, without the authority of the court, to sell or transfer real estate.

Remarks on this enactment.

It is to be regretted that (no doubt owing to want of time at the end of last session) it was not found possible to enact Part I. of this Act in a somewhat fuller form, containing, among other things, well considered and carefully drafted provisions for the guidance of personal representatives as regards their management of and dealings with the real estate of testators or intestate persons. As it is, such guidance must be sought from various and scattered sources, that is to say, from statutes and decisions which were never intended to be applicable to real estate; and, if any question arises as to whether or not a particular statute is applicable to real estate under particular circumstances, personal representatives are left either to decide the question for themselves, and to act accordingly on their own responsibility, or to subject themselves to the trouble, the administration to the delay, and the estate to the expense, of an application to the court for directions as to how to act.

2. Dealings with Real Estate before Probate or Grant of Administration.

It has been seen that an executor derives his authority under the will, and that the estate vests in him as such as from the date of the testator's death (*o*). It follows that he can exercise all powers and do all acts before probate which he would be entitled to do after probate, with certain exceptions as regards actions and suits relating to the estate. Inasmuch, then, as by the Act of 1897 an executor may deal with the real estate of his testator as if such estate were a chattel real, it would seem that the executor may, immediately upon the testator's death, enter upon and take possession of the real estate (*p*). So also he will apparently be able before probate to sell or otherwise dispose of the real

What acts an executor may do before probate.

(*o*) See *ante*, p. 18.   (*p*) See as to chattels, Wentw Off. Ex. 81, 82.

estate, and to give a good title and effectually convey the property to a purchaser or mortgagee (*q*), and give a receipt for the purchase or mortgage money; to assent to the taking of the property by or to convey the same to the devisee or heir-at-law (*r*); and such assent will be good even though it be to a devise to the executor himself (*s*). Production of the probate will, however, be necessary to give a valid title to a purchaser or devisee (*t*). An executor may, before probate, make a valid demise of the lands of his testator (*u*), and may distrain for rent due from a tenant of such lands (*x*).

Death of executor before probate.

If an executor should die without proving the will, any of such acts done by him will be valid (*y*). So where the executor of a tenant for a term of years died before probate, it was held that the term was legally vested in him, and passed, on his death, to his executor. So also, an assent given is not invalidated by the death of the executor before probate (*z*).

Actions before probate.

An executor cannot in his representative character maintain an action before probate (*a*); and even as regards actions brought by him in reliance on his constructive possession as executor, but not naming himself as such, he may be compelled to produce the probate at the hearing in order to prove his title (*b*).

What acts an administrator may do before grant of administration.

Inasmuch as an administrator derives his estate and authority entirely from his appointment by the court (*c*), the powers of an administrator over the real estate of a

---

(*q*) *Brazier* v. *Hudson*, 8 Sim. 67. See *Comber's case*, 1 P. Wms. 768; *Elwood* v. *Christy*, 17 C. B. (N.S.) 754.

(*r*) *Wankford* v. *Wankford*, 1 Salk. 306.

(*s*) Dyer, 367a. *Rex* v. *Stone*, 6 T. R. 298; *Fenton* v. *Clegg*, 9 Exch. 680.

(*t*) *Newton* v. *Metropolitan Rail. Co.*, 1 Dr. & Sm. 583.

(*u*) *Roe* v. *Summersett*, 2 W. Blackst. 692.

(*x*) *Whitehead* v. *Taylor*, 10 A. & E. 210.

(*y*) Wentw. Off. Ex. 82; *Brazier* v. *Hudson*, *supra*.

(*z*) See cases in text in notes (*d*) and (*e*).

(*a*) *Webb* v. *Adkins*, 14 C. B. 401; *Tarn* v. *Commercial Bank of Sydney*, 12 Q. B. D. 294.

(*b*) *Hunt* v. *Stevens*, 2 Taunt. 113.

(*c*) See *ante*, p. 18.

deceased person by virtue of the Act of 1897 will be more restricted than those of an executor as regards dealings with the estate before administration; and it would make no difference in this respect whether he is an administrator of an intestate or administrator with the will annexed (*d*). Thus he will apparently be unable effectually to sell and convey any part of the real estate (*e*). So also it was held that a mortgage of a term of years made by an administrator before letters did not bind the property (*f*).

So also, generally speaking, an agreement with relation to the estate, entered into before grant of administration, is not specifically enforceable against the administrator (*g*).

Again, it would seem that, notwithstanding the rule laid down by the Judicature Act, 1875 (*h*), in case of conflict between law and equity, the latter should prevail, an administrator will not be able to commence an action to maintain a legal right with regard to the real estate of the deceased unless he has previously obtained a grant of administration, for he has no right of action at law until he has obtained it (*i*). If, however, his rights are equitable only, it would seem that he may commence his action, provided he obtains letters of administration before the hearing (*k*).

Actions before administration.

(*d*) *Phillips* v. *Hartley*, 3 C. & P. 121.
(*e*) Preston Abstr. Vol. 3, p. 146. See *Bacon* v. *Simpson*, 3 M. & W. 87; *Morgan* v. *Thomas*, 8 Exch. 302.
(*f*) *Metters* v. *Brown*, 1 H. & C. 686.
(*g*) *Doe* v. *Glen*, 1 A. & E. 49.

(*h*) 36 & 37 Vict. c. 56, s. 25 (11).
(*i*) *Martin* v. *Fuller*, Comb. 371; *Wooldridge* v. *Bishop*, 7 B. & Cr. 406.
(*k*) *Fell* v. *Lutwidge*, Barnd. Ch. Ca. 320; *Humphreys* v. *Ingledon*, 1 P. Wms. 743; *Moses* v. *Levy*, 3 Y. & C. 356; *Horner* v. *Horner*, 23 L. J. Ch. 10.

3. Powers of Executors and Administrators to Sell or Mortgage Real Estate.

Chap. V.

The Act of 1897, by enacting that all enactments and rules of law relating to the powers of personal representatives in respect of personal estate shall apply to real estate so far as applicable, introduces an important alteration in the law as to the powers of executors or administrators to raise money for purposes of administration by the sale or mortgage of the land of a deceased person. It will be convenient in this place briefly to state in what cases executors and administrators have hitherto been able effectually to convey freehold lands of a testator or intestate by way of sale or mortgage.

Express powers of real trusts for sale.

The powers of executors to sell real estate arose either under common law powers in wills, or under powers attached to an interest given to them by wills; thus a direction that the executors should sell, or that the land should be sold by the executors, gave them only a common law power; but a devise to the executors in trust to sell, vested the estate in them with the powers of dealing with the same necessary for the performance of their trust (*l*).

Implied powers of sale by charge of debts.

Executors could also sell and give a good discharge for the purchase money where the real estate was charged by the will expressly or by implication with payment of the testator's debts or legacies, or both (*m*). And a gift of real and personal estate, with a direction for payment of debts and legacies, charges them on the realty in aid of the personalty (*n*). This power of sale was, however, merely equitable, so that,

(*l*) Sugd. Pow. 111, 115. See Co. Litt. 113a; *Doe* v. *Shotter*, 8 A. & E. 905; *R.* v. *Wilson*, 9 Jur. (N.S.) 439.
(*m*) *Elliott* v. *Merryman*, 2 Atk. 4; *Stronghill* v. *Anstey*, 1 De G. M. & G. 635; *Robinson* v. *Lowater*, 5 De G. M. & G. 272.
(*n*) *Greville* v. *Browne*, 7 H.L.C. 682; see *Elliot* v. *Dearsley*, 16 Ch. D. 322.

independently of statutory enactment, executors selling thereunder could not pass the legal estate to a purchaser (*o*); but it seems that the executors could compel the persons in whom the legal estate was vested to join in the conveyance for the purpose of passing such estate (*p*). A charge of debts and legacies extended to lands specifically devised (*q*), but a charge of legacies only was restricted to residue (*r*).

Where real estate was devised to trustees subject to a charge of debts, the power of the executors to sell was ousted, and the trustees were the proper persons to sell and convey, and also to receive and give receipts for the purchase money (*s*).

Devise to trustees with charge of debts.

With regard to personalty, including chattels real, it seems consistent with sound principle, and has been repeatedly affirmed by judicial decision, notwithstanding some expressions of contrary opinion (*t*), that executors and administrators having full and absolute power of disposal by way of sale over the assets might raise money required for purposes of administration by mortgaging the assets (*u*). And on the same principle where executors had an implied power of sale over real estate by virtue of a trust or charge for payment of debts or otherwise, it was held that such a power included a power to mortgage, a mortgage being a conditional sale (*v*); unless, indeed, there was a direction

Power of executors to mortgage land.

(*o*) *Doe* v. *Hughes*, 6 Exch. 223; *Kenrick* v. *Lord Beauclerk*, 3 B.&P. 175, 6 R. R. 746; *Shaw* v. *Bonner*, 1 Keen, 576.
(*p*) *Hodgkinson* v. *Quinn*, 1 J. & H. 303.
(*q*) *Mannox* v. *Greener*, L. R. 14 Eq. 456.
(*r*) *Conron* v. *Conron*, 7 H. L. C. 168.
(*s*) *Shaw* v. *Bonner*, 1 Keen, 599; *Stronghill* v. *Anstey*, 1 De G. M. & G. 647; *Colyer* v. *Finch*, 5 H. L. C. 905.

(*t*) *Andrews* v. *Wingley*, 4 Bro. C. C. 138.
(*u*) *Mead* v. *Lord Ossery*, 3 Atk. 239; *Scott* v. *Tyler*, 2 Dick. 725; *M'Leod* v. *Drummond*, 17 Ves. 154; *Re Cooper*, 20 Ch. D. 611.
(*v*) *Mills* v. *Banks*, 3 P. Wms. 9; *Ball* v. *Hains*, 4 My. & Cr. 276; *Page* v. *Cooper*, 16 Beav. 396; *Metcalf* v. *Hutchinson*, 1 Ch. D. 591; *Balfour* v. *Cooper*, 23 Ch. D. 472.

Chap. V.

to sell so worded as to show that the testator's intention was to create a complete conversion (*x*).

Restrictions on powers to sell or mortgage.

A trust, power, or direction to sell or mortgage for payment of debts or legacies might formerly have been imposed or given subject to restrictions, as that the recourse should not be had to the real estate unless the personalty should prove insufficient for such payments, in which case, if the personal estate was sufficient, the purchaser or mortgagee took nothing (*y*); or that estates devised for payment of debts, etc., should be sold or mortgaged in a particular order (*z*).

Powers of executors under Lord St. Leonard's Act.

In order to obviate difficulties which arose as to the power of trustees or executors to sell or mortgage realty by virtue of a charge of debts, etc., it was in substance enacted by section 14 of Lord St. Leonard's Act that where there is a charge of debts, or of a legacy, or of any specific sum of money, on real estate, and the estate so charged is devised to a trustee or trustees for the whole of the testator's estate or interest therein, and there is an express provision made for raising the charge, the trustee or trustees may, notwithstanding any express trusts, raise the money required for payment of the debts, legacy, or specific sum by sale or mortgage of the estate so charged (*a*). By section 16, the same powers are given to executors, where there is no devise in trust. And the same section seems impliedly to enable executors selling to convey the legal estate if vested in the testator at his death by enacting that a sale under the Act " shall operate only on the estate and interest, whether legal or equitable, of the testator, and shall not render it unnecessary to get in any

---

(*x*) *Holdenby* v. *Spofforth*, 1 Beav. 390.

(*y*) *Duke* v. *Ricks*, Cro. Car. 335; see *Grestham* v. *Cotton*, 34 Beav. 615.

(*z*) *Pierce* v. *Scott*, 1 S. & C. Ex. 257.

(*a*) 22 & 23 Vict. c. 35.

POWERS OF SALE AND MORTGAGE.

outstanding legal estate" (*b*). This statutory power of sale is not exerciseable by an administrator (*c*).

CHAP. V.

In cases where the executors had no power to sell real estate, express or implied, it could only be made available for payment of the debts of a deceased owner by invoking the aid of the court in an administrative action.

Sale by court where no power of sale in executors.

By the feudal law, creditors were not allowed to take in execution the real estates of their debtors which were not transferable except by the lord's consent, on the ground that such transfer would be indirectly effected. Later on the lands of a debtor were rendered liable to be taken in execution during his lifetime at the suit of his creditors. But though, as has been seen (*d*), a person might devise his real estate for payment of his debts or charge it therewith, so as impliedly to give to his executors a power of sale over it, yet if he died intestate, or if he made no such provision by his will, the heir or devisee was entitled to take the real estate free from the claims of the creditors.

Real estate formerly not liable to debts.

The Statute of Fraudulent Devises gave to the specialty creditors of a deceased person a right of action against the devisee and heir jointly where the will contained no provision for payment of debts (*e*). The statute 47 Geo. 3, c. 74, s. 2, rendered the real estates of deceased traders liable to their simple contract creditors. This provision was re-enacted by 1 Will. 4, c. 47, which also provided remedies in cases of debts by covenant, and in cases where there was a devisee and no heir, and the last-mentioned statute, as amended by the statute 2 & 3 Vict. c. 60, empowered the court to decree the debtor's real estates to be sold or mortgaged for payment of his debts, and provided that any surplus

Statute of Fraudulent Devises.

(*b*) See Lewin on Trusts, 9th ed., p. 517.
(*c*) *Re Clay and Tetley's Contract*,
16 Ch. D. 3.
(*d*) *Ante*, p. 64.
(*e*) 3 Wm. & M. c. 14.

F 2

moneys so raised should devolve to the same person and belonged to the same persons who would have been entitled to the lands, if not so sold or mortgaged. Under these statutes the specialty creditors and the simple contract creditors entitled to come in thereunder, were held to claim under the will, and were, therefore, entitled to payment *pari passu*, without any preference of the specialty creditors; and they were further held to come in as the will directed, so that if the will declared that the debts should be paid out of the yearly rents, there could be no sale or mortgage (*f*).

Statute 3 & 4 Will. 4, c. 104 To remedy the defects in the foregoing Acts, the statute 3 & 4 Will. 4, c. 104, was passed, whereby the lands of a debtor, whether a trader or not, are made liable in the hands of his heir or devisee as assets in an administration action for the payment of his simple contract debts as well as his specialty debts; and the heir or devisee was rendered liable to all such proceedings at the suit of simple contract creditors as he would have been liable to before the passing of the Act in respect of the lands at the hands of specialty creditors. The Act provided that specialty creditors, where the heir was bound, should be entitled to payment in full before other specialty creditors, and before simple contract creditors should receive any payment in respect of their claims. This statute did not apply to lands which a testator had charged by will or devised subject to payment of his debts.

Freehold estates over which testator has a general power of appointment, and which he appoints by his will, are assets within this statute for payment of his simple contract debts, but are only applicable for that purpose after all the testator's own property, whether real or personal, has been previously so applied (*g*).

(*f*) *Lingard* v. *Earl of Derby*, 1 Bro. C. C. 311; *Earl of Bath* v. *Earl of Bradford*, 2 Ves. Sen. 589.

(*g*) *Fleming* v. *Buchanan*, 3 De G. M. & G. 976; *Re Van Hagan*, 16 Ch. D. 30.

The priority or preference of specialty creditors over simple contract creditors is taken away by the statute 32 & 33 Vict. c. 46; and by section 10 of the Judicature Act, 1875 (*h*), in the administration by the court of an insolvent estate, the rules as to proof for debts in force for the time being under the law of bankruptcy are to prevail and be observed.

No priority of specialty creditors.

The Act of 1897, by vesting in the personal representatives of a deceased person dying in or after January 1st, 1898, all his real estate, except copyholds and customary freeholds, and by giving to them similar powers of disposal over such real estate as they have hitherto had over chattels real, will enable them, without any application to the court by themselves, or by creditors, in their absolute discretion to sell such real estate, or any part thereof, and to effectually convey the legal estate, if vested in the deceased owner at the time of his death, without the concurrence of the devisee or heir, or to mortgage the estate either by way of legal mortgage (*i*) or equitable charge, and that either by actual conveyance or by deposit of deeds (*k*). And it will make no difference in the exercise of the powers of personal representatives to sell or mortgage real estate, as between themselves and a purchaser or mortgagee, whether or not there is a trust or direction for payment of debts or legacies out of the real estate, or a charge of debts or legacies thereon, or in what terms any such trust, direction, or power may be expressed; and any attempt to impose restrictions or conditions on such discretion will be nugatory.

Statutory powers of personal representatives to sell or mortgage real estate.

Inasmuch as copyholds and customary lands, a perfect legal title to which cannot be obtained without admission, are excepted from the operation of the Act

As to copyholds and customary lands.

(*h*) 39 & 39 Vict. c. 77.   (*k*) *Scott* v. *Tyler*, 2 Dick. 724.
(*i*) *Ball* v. *Harris*, 4 My. & Cr. 276.

of 1897 (*l*), it follows that the powers of the executors or administrators of a deceased owner of such lands to sell or mortgage the same will depend upon the former rules of law as laid down by judicial decision or statutory enactment with regard to such powers. And where there is no such power express or implied, an administration action must be brought in order to raise money for payment of debts by sale or mortgage of copyhold or customary lands.

Where a testator authorizes or directs his executors to sell copyholds, the proper mode of conveyance by them is by deed of bargain and sale, and the appointee under such a deed may claim thereunder to be admitted, and one fine only is payable upon the admission; for the appointee takes immediately under the will (*m*), and if the sale is made in good time before the lord is entitled to seize *quousque*, he cannot refuse to admit as tenant the appointee of the executors (*n*). The legal estate, until sale by the executors in such a case, vests in the customary heir, and if he chooses to be admitted, he must pay his own fine.

Sale of real estate by personal representatives. The effect then of the Act of 1897 is to empower the executors or administrators of a deceased person to sell his freehold real estate, although specifically devised, unless they have assented to the devise; but in case they should have so assented, the purchasers should require the concurrence of the devisee (*o*).

Where some of several executors renounce, the other executors may sell (*p*); and if one or more die, the statutory power of sale given by the Act of 1897 may be exercised by the survivors or survivor of them for the time being (*q*).

(*l*) *Ante*, p. 24.
(*m*) *Holder* v. *Preston*, 2 Wils. 400; see Watk. Cop. 105, 127, 334, 353.
(*n*) *Holder* v. *Preston, supra*
(*o*) Dart V. & P.
(*p*) 21 Hen. 8, c. 4.
(*q*) 56 & 57 Vict. c. 53, s. 22.

Personal representatives being by this Act constituted trustees with a power of sale over the real estate, will have in the exercise of such powers the auxiliary powers given by the Trustee Act, 1893 (r), which are as follows :—

> Section 13.—(1.) Where a trust for sale or a power of sale of property is vested in a trustee, he may sell or concur with any other person in selling all or any part of the property, either subject to prior charges or not, and either together or in lots, by public auction or by private contract, subject to any such conditions respecting title or evidence of title or other matter as the trustee thinks fit, with power to vary any contract for sale, and to buy in at any auction, or to rescind any contract for sale and to re-sell, without being answerable for any loss.
>
> (2.) This section applies only if and as far as a contrary intention is not expressed in the instrument creating the trust or power, and shall have effect subject to the terms of that instrument and to the provisions therein contained.

Power of trustee for sale to sell by auction, etc.

By the concluding clause of section 2, sub-section (2), of the Act of 1897 (which is the instrument creating the power of sale of personal representatives over real estate) it is enacted that "it shall not be lawful for some or one only of several joint personal representatives, without the authority of the court, to sell or transfer real estate."

It would obviously be beyond the scope of these notes to discuss in detail the principles which should guide personal representatives, as trustees of real estate vested in them, in the exercise of their statutory power of sale (s); but some of the leading rules on this point may be here briefly noticed.

Exercise of statutory power of sale.

(r) 56 & 57 Vict. c. 53.   (s) See as to this, Lewin on Trusts (9th ed.) ch. xviii.

The personal representatives, in exercising their power of sale, must pay due regard to the purposes of their trust and the interests of the persons interested thereunder. The court will not enforce specific performance of a contract which, on the face of it, shows that those interests are being prejudiced, thereby involving a breach of trust (*t*).

Sale of land and timber separately.
Although section 13 of the Trustee Act, 1893, authorizes a sale of "all or any part of the property," the estate and the timber thereon cannot be sold separately (*u*) except with the sanction of the court (*x*).

Sale of mines and surface separately.
The same rule applies to a sale of the surface of land apart from the mines and minerals thereunder (*y*); but by section 44 of the Trustee Act, 1893, the court has power to sanction a sale by trustees of land or mines and minerals separately from each other.

Sale free from incumbrances.
By section 5 of the Conveyancing and Law of Property Act, 1881 (*z*), where the real estate is subject to prior charges, the real representatives desiring to sell the same may apply to the court for an order directing payment out of the general estate of such a sum as, when invested in Government securities, will be sufficient to provide for the charges and the contingency of further expenses and the conveyance of the land free from such charges.

Mode of sale.
Personal representatives as trustees should use their discretion as to the mode of sale, whether by public auction or private contract, so as to endeavour to sell to the best advantage (*a*). They should cause a valuation

---

(*t*) *Wood* v. *Richardson*, 4 Beav. 176; *White* v. *Cuddon*, 8 Cl. & F. 788; see also cases cited Blyth & Jarm. Conv. (4th ed.) Vol. II. p. 729.
(*u*) *Cholmley* v. *Paxton*, 3 Bing. 207, 5 Bing. 48.
(*x*) See 22 & 23 Vict. c. 35, s. 13.

(*y*) *Buckley* v. *Howell*, 29 Beav. 546.
(*z*) 44 & 45 Vict. c. 41.
(*a*) *Downes* v. *Grazebrook*, 3 Mer. 208; 17 R. R. 62; see *Exp. Dunman*, 2 Rose, 66; *Exp. Harly*, 2 D. & E. 631; *Darey* v. *Durrant*, 1 De G. & J. 535.

to be made by a competent surveyor or valuer so as to guide them as to what is a proper price for them to accept (b).

Sales under depreciatory conditions.

As regards sales under depreciatory conditions, trustees have always been allowed a fair discretion, even as against their *cestuis que trusts*, and it has been held, independently of statutory enactments, conditions that even of a special character are not lightly to be deemed to be of such a depreciatory character as to render personal representatives selling under such conditions liable to the persons entitled for breach of trust or an objection to title (c). And as regards such conditions amounting to a breach of trust as between a trustee and his *cestuis que trust*, or an objection to title so as to entitle a *cestuis que trust* or purchaser to set aside the sale, section 14 of the Trustee Act, 1893, enacts as follows:—

Power to sell subject to depreciatory conditions.

(1.) No sale made by a trustee shall be impeached by any beneficiary upon the ground that any of the conditions subject to which the sale was made may have been unnecessarily depreciatory, unless it also appears that the consideration for the sale was thereby rendered inadequate.

(2.) No sale made by a trustee shall, after the execution of the conveyance, be impeached as against the purchaser upon the ground that any of the conditions subject to which the sale was made may have been unnecessarily depreciatory, unless it appears that the purchaser was acting in collusion with the trustee at the time when the contract for sale was made.

(3.) No purchaser, upon any sale made by a trustee, shall be at liberty to make any objection against the title upon the ground aforesaid.

Personal representatives mortgaging

It is now settled that personal representatives or trustees, having power to mortgage such estate, are

---

(b) *Fry* v. *Tapson*, 28 Ch. D. 568.
(c) Sugd. V. & P. 63; see *Hudson* v. *Bell*, 2 Beav. 17; *Hyde* v. *Dallaway*, 4 Beav. 606; *Morley* v. *Cook*, 2 Ha. 106.

CHAP. V.
may give power of sale.
Rate of interest.

authorized to give to the mortgagee a power of sale (d); a power of sale is now implied in every mortgage made by deed, unless expressly excluded (e).

The personal representatives having power to mortgage the real estate of their testator or intestate, will have power to charge the property with interest on the money advanced until repayment, at any rate which may be agreed upon, not necessarily restricted to the rate of interest usually allowed by the court (f).

Purchaser or mortgagee not liable to see to application of money.

It seems clear that the rule, which has hitherto prevailed where real estate is subject to a charge of debts, will apply to sales and mortgages of real estates by personal representatives in due course of administration under the Act of 1897; that is to say, that purchasers and mortgagees will not be bound to see to the application of the money, but will be discharged from any such liability by the receipt of the personal representatives, on the ground that, in the absence of evidence to the contrary, they must be presumed to have raised the money by sale or mortgage for purposes of administration (g). If, however, the circumstances of the transaction are such as to affect the purchaser or mortgagee with actual or constructive notice that the money is required, not for purposes of administration, but for the personal representatives' own purposes, the sale or mortgage will be liable to be set aside at the instance of the beneficiaries (h). Inasmuch as it is presumed that executors or administrators selling the property are doing so for payment of debts, a purchaser is not concerned or entitled to inquire whether any debts remain unpaid, unless twenty years have elapsed since the death (i).

(d) *Lewis* v. *Freke*, 2 Ves. Jun. 507; 2 R. R. 301. See *Lord Kilmurry* v. *Geary*, 2 Salk. 538; *Boycott* v. *Cotton*, 1 Atk. 552; *Hall* v. *Carter*, 2 Atk. 358.
(e) *Russell* v. *Plaice*, 18 Beav. 21; *Re Chawners' Will*, L. R. 8 Eq. 569; *Cruikshank* v. *Duffin*, L. R. 13 Eq. 555.

(f) 44 & 45 Vict c. 41, s. 19.
(g) *Ithell* v. *Beane*, 1 Ves. Sen. 215; *Barker* v. *Duke of Devonshire*, 3 Mer. 310.
(h) *Hill* v. *Simpson*, 7 Ves. 152; *Watkins* v. *Cheek*, 2 S. & St. 205.
(i) *Re Tanqueray-Willaume and Landau*, 20 Ch. D. 465.

4. Powers of Executors and Administrators as to Leasing and Management of Real Estate during the Period of Administration.

Although, as will be seen hereafter (*k*), the court may, after the expiration of a year from the death of a testator or intestate, on the application of a person beneficially entitled, order the real representatives to convey the real estate, or so much thereof as shall not have been disposed of in course of administration, to such person, yet it may happen that, owing to the complication of the affairs of the deceased, or for other reasons, it may be found impossible to complete the administration within that period. It therefore becomes natural to consider what will be the powers of personal representatives as to management of the property, and application of the rents and profits, while they retain possession, and before they assent to the devise or convey the property to the devisee or heir. In this connection, it is important to bear in mind that by section 2, sub-section (1), of the Act of 1897, the personal representatives are expressly declared to be trustees for the persons by law entitled thereto (*l*).

In like manner as executors or administrators, where the circumstances of the case render it necessary or expedient in the interests of the estate and of the persons entitled thereto, may grant underleases of leaseholds forming part of the estate of a deceased person (*m*), it seems clear that real representatives may now, by virtue of the Act of 1897, under similar circumstances, grant leases of his freeholds, and that the rents reserved by such leases will be assets in their hands to be applied in due course of administration. But on this point,

Powers of leasing.

(*k*) *Post*, p. 110.
(*l*) *Ante*, p. 52.

(*m*) Bac. Abr., tit. Leases (I) 7; Williams, Executors, Vol. I., p. 808.

CHAP. V.

JESSEL, M.R., observed as follows (n):—"An administrator is considered in a court of equity as a trustee, and his primary duty is to sell the intestate's estate for payment of his debts. It is quite true that, having the legal estate in the leaseholds, he may in some cases underlet them, and the underlease will be supported in equity as well as at law. But that is an exceptional mode of dealing with the assets, and those who accept the title must take it subject to the question whether it was the best way of administering the assets." As the Act of 1897 does not contain any express exemption of persons taking leases from personal representatives from such liability, it would seem that this rule will apply in such cases, so that leases by personal representatives will require justification, if challenged. It is, however, obvious that it may often happen that a lease of real estate, and application of the rents towards the payment of the debts of the deceased owner, may be a better mode of administering the estate than a sale, as being more advantageous to the interests of the beneficiary (o).

What demises may be made by personal representatives.

Inasmuch as the Act of 1897 expressly declares that personal representatives shall be trustees for the persons entitled (p), it seems clear that they may continue existing tenancies or grant fresh tenancies of vacant lands from year to year (q), as otherwise the estate might be rendered unproductive in their hands; but it seems doubtful whether they can, in the absence of express powers, grant in their character of trustees leases for longer than a year (r), unless under exceptional circumstances (s); and, if they grant a lease for a term of years, the onus would apparently rest on them and on the lessee taking under them of showing that

(n) *Oceanic Steam Navigation Co.* v. *Sutherberry*, 16 Ch. D. 236, at p. 243.
(o) See *Keating* v. *Lloyd*, 1 Ll. & G. 133.
(p) *Ante*, p. 52.

(q) *Fitzpatrick* v. *Waring*, 11 L. R. Ir. 35.
(r) *Re Shaw*, L. R. 12 Eq. 124.
(s) *Naylor* v. *Arnett*, 1 Russ. & My. 501. See *Wood* v. *Patteson*, 10 Beav. 541.

the act was reasonable, and done in the fair management of the estate (*t*). The court has refused to sanction a mining lease by trustees for sixty years (*u*), or a lease by them of unopened mines (*x*).

CHAP. V.

Trustees having a general power to lease may grant a lease to a corporation or limited company (*y*).

Lease to corporation.

A lease granted by a personal representative must not contain any unusual provisions detrimental to the inheritance, as for instance, a proviso giving an option of purchase to the lessee (*z*).

Option of purchase.

It would seem that personal representatives, if and so far as empowered to grant leases in their capacity of trustees, may let the property upon leases granted partly in consideration of a covenant by the lessee to do all repairs which may be necessary during the term (*a*).

Repairing leases.

Personal representatives will be competent and compellable to grant (*b*) or renew (*c*) a lease pursuant to a covenant or agreement in that behalf made or entered into by the deceased owner in his lifetime.

Lease pursuant to contract by deceased owner.

As a lessee is estopped from denying his lessor's title (*d*), it is obvious that the only persons who can claim to set aside the lease are the devisee or heir or those claiming under him. And accordingly if personal representatives think it advisable to grant a lease for a term of years, they should obtain the concurrence of the

Concurrence of heir or devisee.

(*t*) *Att.-Gen.* v. *Owen,* 10 Ves. 560.
(*u*) *Wood* v. *Patteson, supra.*
(*x*) *Clegg* v. *Rowland,* L. R. 2 Eq. 160.
(*y*) *Re Jeffcock,* 51 L. J. Ch. 507. See *Pharmaceutical Society* v. *London, etc., Supply Association,* 5 App. Cas. 857.
(*z*) *Oceanic Steam Navigation Co.* v. *Sutherberry,* 16 Ch. D. 236. See *Salamon* v. *Sopwith,* 53 L. T. (N.S.) 826.

(*a*) *Easton* v. *Pratt,* 2 H. & C. 676; *Truscott* v. *Diamond Rock Boring Co.* 20 Ch. D. 251.
(*b*) *Davis* v. *Harforde,* 22 Ch. D. 128.
(*c*) *Macartney* v. *Blundell,* 2 Ridgw. P. C. 113.
(*d*) *Cooke* v. *Loxley,* 5 T. R. 4; *Cuthbertson* v. *Irving,* 4 H. & N. 742; *Becket* v. *Bradley,* 7 M. & G. 994; 8 Scott N. R. 843; *Langford* v. *Selmes,* 3 K. & J. 220; *Delany* v. *Fox,* 1 C. B. (N.S.) 166; 2 *ibid,* 768.

devisee or heir for the purpose of signifying his approval and confirmation of the lease; this will also prevent any question arising as to the executors having assented to the devise before the granting of the lease. A person taking a lease from executors or administrators should always require such concurrence or the sanction of the court.

Powers of management.

Where subject to the intermediate vesting of the legal estate in personal representatives for purposes of administration, an estate of inheritance in freeholds devolves by will or under an intestacy upon a devisee or heir, the position of affairs as to the management of the estate until assent or conveyance to the person entitled seems not to be altogether free from complication, and to require some consideration in detail.

Powers of real representatives to distrain for rents.

The executors or administrators, unless they convey the property by way of sale or legal mortgage, will be at law the owners thereof. If, therefore, an owner of land lets it and dies, his real representatives will be legally entitled to the freehold reversion, in like manner as executors have been and are entitled to the leasehold reversion of property which has been underlet by their testator (*e*), together with the rents annexed to the freehold reversion; and accordingly they may by the common law distrain for arrears of rent accrued due during the lifetime of the deceased (*f*), and also for rents accruing due so long as they continue in possession of the property, such right being inherent to their legal ownership (*g*).

As to land, etc., in occupation of deceased.

If the real estate of a deceased person consists wholly or in part of land on which buildings are

---

(*e*) Williams, Executors (9th ed.), Vol. I., p. 796.
(*f*) *Wade* v. *Marsh*, 1 Roll. Abr. 672; tit. Distress, (O) 13. See also Statutes 32 Hen. 8, c. 37 and 3 & 4 Will. 4, c. 42, s. 37.; and see Williams on Executors (9th ed.) Vol. I., pp. 97—801.
(*g*) *Whitehead* v. *Taylor*, 10 A. & E. 210 (distress before probate).

erected or in course of erection, or of mines which he worked himself, or of premises in which he carried on a trade or business, the real representatives would seem to be placed in a position of considerable responsibility and difficulty.

It is conceived that personal representatives during their period of possession will, like ordinary trustees, be justified in laying out rents and profits in repair of existing buildings, such as are absolutely necessary for the preservation of the property from deterioration (*h*); and it would seem that they may cut timber on the lands for the purpose of such repairs (*i*). But they will not, as a general rule, be allowed for lasting improvements (*k*), or re-building (*l*), still less for repairs which are merely decorative (*m*), unless made with the consent of the devisee or heir.

Repairs and improvements.

Where a lease granted by a deceased owner contains a covenant by the lessor and his heirs, etc., to keep the premises in repair during the term, it seems clear that the liability under the covenant which would otherwise have bound the heir or devisee will now attach to the personal representatives during their possession, independently of the personal liability under the covenant which formerly devolved on the executors as such (*n*).

Liability under covenant to repair.

With respect to working mines comprised in the real estate of a deceased person, there appear to be few reported cases which afford any assistance for the guidance of personal representatives in their administration of real estate. The reason for this is probably that owners of mines being generally men of business

As to mines and minerals.

(*h*) *Caldecott* v. *Brown*, 2 Ha. 145; *Maclaren* v. *Stainton*, M.R. March 14th, 1866, not reported.

(*i*) Lewin on Trusts (9th ed.) pp. 643, 646. See *Att.-Gen.* v. *Geary*, 3 Mer. 513.

(*k*) *Nairn* v. *Majoribanks*, 3 Russ. 582.

(*l*) *Bleazard* v. *Whalley*, 2 Eq. Rep. 1093. See *Drake* v. *Trefusis*, L. R. 10 Ch. A. 364.

(*m*) *Bridge* v. *Brown*, 2 Y & C. C. C. 181.

(*n*) *Tremere* v. *Morrison*, 1 Bing. N. S. 89.

CHAP. V.

habits, whether their interests are in freehold or leasehold mines, give by their wills appropriate and carefully considered powers and provisions for the management of such property by their executors or trustees.

It would seem, however, that personal representatives, being trustees for the persons entitled, may work open gravel pits, quarries or mines for the benefit of their *cestuis que trusts* (o), who are in the first place the creditors, and in the next place the devisee or heir.

As to timber.

It would also seem that executors or administrators, being in the position of trustees with a general control over the real estate, may cut decaying timber and sell it and apply the proceeds for the purposes of their trust (p); also that they may cut timber and underwood in the proper course of thinning plantations (q).

As to premises employed in trade or business.

As a general rule it has been held, that executors or administrators are not justified in continuing, at the expense of the personal estate, a trade or business carried on by the testator or intestate during his lifetime (r), unless and except so far as they are positively and distinctly authorized to do so by the will (s), or except so far as such continuance is absolutely necessary to prevent material injury to the estate; and the same rule, as it is conceived, will equally apply to the case of freeholds which have been held and employed by a deceased person for the purposes of his trade or business, and continue to be held and employed by his personal representatives for those purposes.

If an executor or administrator, without express authority and on insufficient grounds, carries on a trade

---

(o) *Cowley* v. *Wellesley*, 35 Beav. 638; *Elias* v. *Snowden Slate Co.*, 4 App. Cas. 454.
(p) *Waldo* v. *Waldo*, 7 Sim. 261; 12 Sim. 107.
(q) *Cowley* v. *Wellesley*, supra;

see *Honeywood* v. *Honeywood*, L. R. 18 Eq. 306.
(r) *Burker* v. *Barker*, 1 T. R. 295; *Exp. Garland*, 10 Ves. 119.
(s) *Per* Lord LANGDALE in *Kirkman* v. *Booth*, 11 Beav. 273, 820.

or business unless with the sanction of the court, he will incur serious responsibility, for he will not be allowed to derive any personal benefit, if the venture proves profitable; but in case of loss he will be personally liable for debts contracted in carrying on the business as from the testator's death to the extent of all his own property. He may be made a bankrupt in respect of his liability for such losses, and both the creditors and the legatees may prove in such bankruptcy against his own estate, leaving the remainder of the assets of the deceased trader free and unaffected by the bankruptcy to be distributed amongst the legatees or next-of-kin unaffected by such bankruptcy (*t*).

It may be suggested that, having regard to the form in which this part of the Act is passed, it will be advisable that land owners, in all cases where it is likely that recourse may be had to their real estate for purposes of administration, should by their wills give express directions to their executors as regards the control, management, and dealings generally with the real estate. It need hardly be said that the drafting of provisions conferring such powers and authorities, or giving such directions, will in many cases require much care and consideration of the circumstances of the particular case, and clearness and nicety of expression. Forms of similar provisions giving similar powers and directions to executors as regards chattels real, and to trustees as regards real estate generally, will be found in various text books, and may be adapted for use in the case of real representatives (*u*).

Advisability of express testamentary provisions as to management.

(*t*) *Exp. Garland, supra* ; *Exp. Richardson,* 1 Buck. 209 ; *Owen* v. *Delamere,* L. R. 15 Eq. 134 ; *Fairland* v. *Percy,* L. R. 3 P. & D. 217. See Williams on Executors (9th ed.) Vol. II., p. 1682.

(*u*) Byth. & Jarm. Conv. (4th ed.) Vol. VII., pp. 777, 778 (business), 919, 920 (management generally), 921—923 (mining and building leases), 1010, 1011 (management of farm); King & Elph. Conv. (4th ed.) Vol. II., pp. 841, 842 (management generally), 653, 683, (leases), 843 (management of farm).

CHAPTER VI.

RIGHTS, DUTIES, AND LIABILITIES OF PERSONAL REPRESENTATIVES IN RESPECT OF REAL ESTATE.

1. Duty of Personal Representatives is to Pay Debts and Deliver Property so far as not required for such Payment, to the Persons entitled thereto.

Payment of debts is the primary duty of personal representatives.

In the administration of assets, whether real or personal, all the debts or liabilities of the deceased person must first be paid or provided for, before an executor is justified in paying or transferring any legacy or devise whether general or specific. If, therefore, an executor acting *bonâ fide* and under a conviction that the assets are amply sufficient for payment of the the testator's debts, permits specific legatees to retain or possess themselves of the property bequeathed to them, he will be answerable for the value of that property, with interest at 4 per cent., if there ultimately be a deficiency in the assets, although the deficiency should be occasioned by subsequent events which the executor or administrator had no reason to anticipate; and the court will direct an account of the value of the property so possessed by the legatees, and interest to be computed unless it is certain that the assets will be ultimately sufficient to satisfy the creditors (*x*).

As to contingent debts and liabilities.

The liability of an executor paying a legacy or share of residue extends to cases where he has notice of a

(*x*) *Spode* v. *Smith*, 4 Russ. 511. See *Davies* v. *Nicholson*, 2 De G. & J. 693.

contingent or possible legacy which may ripen into a contingent claim (y), and even if the testator's estate is subject to any debt or claim of which the executor has no notice, he will continue liable to satisfy such debt or claim to the extent of the assets originally in his hands if he has paid or transferred them to the persons entitled thereto under the will (z), unless, indeed, on the ground of *laches*, the creditor should be held to be precluded from prosecuting his claim (a).

Executors are to some extent relieved from this liability by the statute 22 & 23 Vict. c. 35, s. 29, which in effect provides that after giving such notices as would be given by an order of the court in an administration action to creditors and others to send in their claims, an executor shall not be liable in respect of such claim of which he had not then notice, but may proceed to a distribution of the assets without prejudice to the right of creditors to follow the assets after distribution. {Statutory notice to creditors protects personal representatives.}

The rules of law above stated which have prevailed with regard to bequests of personalty will now apply to devises, whether specific or general, of real estate, so as to render it unsafe for the personal representatives of a deceased to assent to a devise contained in his will, or to convey the property to the devisee, until they are satisfied that all claims and debts against the estate are paid or fully provided for. {Personal representatives shall not assent to devise till debts are paid or provided for.}

Corresponding to the duty of personal representatives in the first place to pay all the debts of the deceased, and to their liability if they fail in such duty, they have {Right of personal representatives to indemnity on assenting to a devise.}

(y) *Rector* v. *Gennet*, Cro. Eliz. 466; *Hawkins* v. *Day*, Ambl. 160; *Pearson* v. *Archdeacon*, L. R. 10 Eq. 477.
(z) *Norman* v. *Baldry*, 6 Sim. 621; *Smith* v. *Day*, 2 M. & W. 684; *Knatchbull* v. *Fearnhead*, 3 My. & Cr. 122; *Hill* v. *Gomme*, 1 Beav. 540.
(a) *Davis* v. *Blackwell*, 9 Bing. 5. See *Rhodes* v. *Brown*, 2 Bing. N. S. 493. See also Williams on Executors (9th ed.), Vol. II., p. 1206.

the right, where such liability exists or if there are reasonable grounds for supposing that it may exist, to refuse to part with the assets, *i.e.*, in the case of real estate, to assent to a devise, specific or general, or to convey the property to the heir-at-law, without a sufficient indemnity, either personal or by way of adequate security charged upon the property (*b*). In cases of doubt, it is always prudent for a personal representative, before parting with the property, to apply for an order of the court directing him how to act, which will effectually protect him from all liability in the matter (*c*).

Transfer of real estate not required for administration to devisee.

The executors of a will devising real estate, having provided for the payment of debts and liabilities of a deceased owner of real estate, and, if and so far as necessary for that purpose, sold or mortgaged the land or appropriated the rents and profits accruing during the period of administration, and having also (as it would seem) paid or provided for legacies, if any (*d*), must next transfer the property by assent or conveyance to the devisee under the will.

Whether on intestacy, real estate not required for administration must be transferred to heir, or goes among next-of-kin.

In the case of an intestacy of an owner of freehold real estate, it is conceived, and has been assumed throughout these notes, that the administrators, after providing for the debts and liabilities, will hold the property in trust for the heir-at-law as being the person "by law beneficially entitled thereto." But that this is so is not rendered by the Act of 1897 as clear as might have been desired; indeed, upon a strict construction of the Act in such case, the real estate, so far as not applied in due course of administration, would go to the next-of-kin, inasmuch as by section 2, sub-

---

(*b*) *Simmonds* v. *Bolland*, 3 Mer. 547; *Cochrane* v. *Robinson*, 11 Sim. 378; *Hickling* v. *Boyer*, 3 Mac. & Y. 635; *Dean* v. *Allen*, 20 Beav. 1.

(*c*) *Dean* v. *Allen*, *supra*; *England* v. *Tredegar*, L. R. 1 Eq. 344.

(*d*) See *post*, p. 92.

section (3), of the Act (e), real estate is to be administered "with the same incidents as if it were personal estate," and one of the best known "incidents" of the administration of personal estate is that the unapplied residue is distributable among the statutory next-of-kin. No saving clause preserving the right of the heir is inserted in the Act, and in the sub-section referred to, the words "so far as the same are applicable," which occur elsewhere in the Act (*f*), are not inserted. Moreover, by section 4, sub-section (1), of the Act (*g*), personal representatives are empowered with the consent of the person entitled to a share of residue, but without the consent of the devisee or heir, to appropriate any part of the residuary estate to satisfy the share; it may be, however, that these words are to be read distributively, so as to empower personal representatives to appropriate residuary personal estate to satisfy shares of residuary personalty whether passing by a bequest or under an intestacy, and to appropriate real residue to answer shares in such residue only where the same is devised to several persons as joint tenants or where it passes under an intestacy to several heirs in gavelkind or co-parceners. It has been seen, moreover, that the Act gives to the heir, if not also one of the next-of-kin, an equal right with the next-of-kin to a grant of administration, and by section 3, sub-section (1), the personal representatives are empowered to convey the land "to any person entitled thereto as *heir*, devisee, or otherwise." It is therefore conceived that the intention of the Legislature and the consequent effect of the Act must be that, in case of intestacy, the heir should retain some estate or interest in the land, which estate or interest can only be that to which he was entitled before the Act, except so far as expressly

(e) *Post*, p. 90.   (g) *Post*, p. 112.
(f) See s. 2 (2), *ante*, p. 60.

and positively interfered with or suspended by the Act. The question cannot, however, be regarded as absolutely free from doubt.

2. Liability of Personal Representatives for their Acts and Defaults in Administering Real Estate.

This subject must here be treated very briefly, and only with special reference to the administration of real estate (*h*).

Liability for breach of trust.

An executor or administrator accepting his office as such is personally liable in equity for all breaches of any trusts which are incident to his office (*i*); and where an executor is also devisee in trust under a will, his acceptance of the executorship, either by proving the will, or by intermeddling with the estate, will be deemed to be an acceptance of all trusts conveyed to the devisee, and render him liable for breach of any of such special trusts (*k*).

Personal representatives must manage estate for benefit of persons entitled.

Personal representatives being expressly declared to be trustees, as regards the real estate, for the persons beneficially entitled thereto, will be bound to manage the estate, so far as their powers will admit of their doing so, to the best possible advantage for the benefit of those persons.

Personal representatives not allowed any remuneration for trouble.

They will not be allowed to make any profit for themselves out of their trust; and, accordingly, however onerous the duties of management of the estate may be, they will not be entitled to any remuneration

---

(*h*) See as to *devastavit* or misconduct of personal representatives generally, Williams on Executors (9th ed.), Vol. II, pp. 1690 *et seq.*

(*i*) *Re Marsden*, 26 Ch. D. 783, 789.

(*k*) *Mucklow* v. *Fuller*, Jac. 198; *Booth* v. *Booth*, 1 Beav. 125; *Williams* v. *Nixon*, 2 Beav. 472.

for their trouble, or to any allowance beyond necessary and proper expenses actually paid by them, unless the will expressly provided for their remuneration (*l*). A plea that they derive no benefit from their office, but that it is merely honorary, is no excuse for want of fidelity and diligence in carrying out the duties of their trust (*m*). The fact that by their diligence and exertions the value of the estate has been preserved or increased, gives them no claim to remuneration (*n*); and, if they retain out of the rents and profits any compensation or remuneration for their trouble and services, they will be compellable to refund it (*o*).

Employment of agents

Personal representatives may, however, employ solicitors to do their legal business (*p*), and stewards or bailiffs (*q*), and agents to collect rents, if such collection be troublesome (*r*), at the expense of the estate; but they must use their reasonable discretion as to the amount of remuneration to be allowed for such services (*s*).

Liability of personal representatives for waste.

It would seem that personal representatives, as regards real estate vested in them, will be liable, if, by reason of want of caution or diligence in their dealings, they cause the estate to be wasted (*t*); as, for instance, if they grossly misconduct the cultivation of the land, or refuse or remove a solvent and respectable tenant (*u*),

---

(*l*) *Robinson* v. *Pett*, 3 P. Wms. 132; 2 Wh. & Tud. L. C. Eq. 214; *Brocksopp* v. *Barnes*, 5 Marshl. 90. See *Moore* v. *Frowd*, 2 My. & Cr. 45; *Re Barber*, 34 Ch. D. 77, 81; *Re Corsellis*, 34 Ch. D. 675, 684.

(*m*) *Charitable Corporation* v. *Sutton*, 2 Atk. 405.

(*n*) *Robinson* v. *Pett*, *supra*; *Longstaffe* v. *Fenwick*, 10 Ves. 404, 8 R. R. 8.; *Barrett* v. *Hartley*, L. R. 2 Eq. 789.

(*o*) *Re Bedingfield*, 57 L. T. (N.S.) 332.

(*p*) *Re Weall*, 42 Ch. D. 674, 677.

(*q*) *Re Whiteley*, *Whiteley* v. *Serroyal*, 12 App. Cas. 727.

(*r*) *Godfrey* v. *Watson*, 3 Atk. 518 (mortgagee in possession).

(*s*) *Re Weall*, *supra*, at p. 678. See *Speight* v. *Gaunt*, 9 App. Cas. 1.

(*t*) See *Rowley* v. *Adams*, 2 H. L. C. 725; *Buxton* v. *Buxton*, 1 My. & Cr. 80.

(*u*) *Wragg* v. *Denham*, 2 Y. & C. Ex. 117; *Anon*, 1 Vern. 45; *Hughes* v. *Williams*, 12 Ves. 493, 8 R. R. 364 (cases of mortgagee in possession).

but that they will not be liable for mere permissive waste, as neglecting to keep buildings in proper repair (*x*).

Personal representatives bound to give full information.

Personal representatives being trustees of the real estate for the persons beneficially entitled thereto, will be bound to give to such persons full information as to their dealings with, and other matters relating to the estate (*y*), and to produce for the inspection of the beneficiaries all title deeds in their hands (*z*), and communications with solicitors (*a*), and cases and opinions of counsel (*b*) not made or taken after the commencement of an action.

Liability of personal representatives to account.

It is well settled that it is the bounden duty of an executor or administrator to keep clear and accurate accounts of his administration of the property, and to be always ready to render such accounts when called upon to do so (*c*). If an action is rendered necessary by reason of their refusal to render proper accounts, they may be liable in costs, even though they allege that nothing is due from them, which turns out to be the fact (*d*). It will be no excuse for failure to keep and produce proper accounts that the personal representatives are charged with breach of trust (*e*), nor that they are inexperienced in keeping accounts and therefore unable to do so, for in such a case it would be their right and duty to employ a competent accountant at the expense of the estate (*f*). They cannot attach to their compliance with a request to furnish accounts any condition, such as that they shall be allowed expenses

---

(*x*) *Powys* v. *Blagrave*, 4 De. G. M. & G. 448.

(*y*) *Ryder* v. *Bickerton*, 3 Swanst. 81.

(*z*) *Davis* v. *Dysart*, 20 Beav. 414; *Re Cowin*, 33 Ch. D. 179.

(*a*) *Re Mason*, 22 Ch. D. 609; *Re Postlethwaite*, 35 Ch. D. 722.

(*b*) *Wynne* v. *Hamberston*, 27 Beav. 421; *Talbot* v. *Marshfield*, 2 Dr. & Sm. 285.

(*c*) *Freeman* v. *Fairlie*, 3 Mer. 29, at pp. 43, 44; *Pearse* v. *Green*, 135, 140.

(*d*) *Newton* v. *Askew*, 11 Beav. 145, 152; *Eglin* v. *Sanderson*, 3 Giff. 434.

(*e*) *Henry* v. *Macdonald*, 15 W. R. 165.

(*f*) *Wroe* v. *Seed*, 4 Giff. 425, 429. See *New* v. *Jones*, 1 Mac. & G. 668 n; *Henderson* v. *McIver*, 3 Madd. 275.

not legally chargeable (*g*); but an executor, even though a solicitor, has been held to be entitled to be guaranteed against the costs of taking the accounts before rendering them (*h*).

Personal representatives must account for all rents and profits accruing during the period of administration from the real estate of the deceased (*i*). So if they allow one of their number to occupy a house on the estate at less than a fair rent, they will be chargeable with the fair rent (*k*).

Accounts of rents and profits.

Personal representatives who act in good faith and to the best of their judgment in the administration of real estate, of which they are by the Act of 1897 expressly declared to be trustees (*l*), will apparently be entitled as such trustees to claim the protection afforded by the Judicial Trustees Act (*m*), which enacts as follows :—

Protection of personal representatives acting in good faith.

> Section 3.—(1.) If it appears to the Court that a trustee, whether appointed under this Act or not, is or may be personally liable for any breach of trust, whether the transaction alleged to be a breach of trust occurred before or after the passing of this Act, but has acted honestly and reasonably, and ought fairly to be excused for the breach of trust, and for omitting to obtain the directions of the Court in the matter in which he committed such breach, then the Court may relieve the trustee, either wholly or partly, from personal liability for the same.

Jurisdiction of court in cases of breach of trust.

No general rules or principles can be laid down to be acted on in carrying out the provisions of this section, and each case must depend on its own circumstances; but the court must be satisfied, before exercising the powers conferred on it, by sufficient evidence, that the trustees acted reasonably (*n*).

(*g*) *Underwood* v. *Trower*, W. N. (1867) 83.
(*h*) *Re Bosworth*, 58 L. J. Ch. 432.
(*i*) Godolphin, Part II., ch. 24, s. 21.
(*k*) *De Cordova* v. *De Cordova*, 9 App. Cas. 733.
(*l*) *Ante* p. 52.
(*m*) 59 & 60 Vict. c. 35.
(*n*) *Re Turner*, [1897] 1 Ch. 536.

CHAPTER VII.

APPLICATION OF ESTATE IN THE ADMINISTRATION OF THE ASSETS OF A DECEASED PERSON.

1. GENERAL STATUTORY RULE AS TO ADMINISTRATION OF REAL ESTATE.

Administration of real estate as personal estate.

SECTION 2, sub-section (3) of the Act of 1897 enacts that—

> "In the administration of the assets of a person dying after the commencement of this Act, his real estate shall be administered in the same manner, subject to the same liabilities for debt, costs, and expenses, and with the same incidents, as if it were personal estate; provided that nothing herein contained shall alter or affect the order in which real and personal assets respectively are now applicable in or towards the payment of funeral and testamentary expenses, debts, or legacies, or the liability of real estate to be charged with the payment of legacies."

A detailed examination of all the rules which have hitherto prevailed in the administration of assets with regard to personal estate, and which are now by this sub-section made applicable by real estate, would be beyond the scope and limits of the present treatise. It must therefore suffice in this place very briefly to notice the liabilities and incidents referred to in this sub-section.

Purchasers need not inquire as to necessity for sale.

The effect of the above enactment, having regard to the proviso at the end, appears to be, that a purchaser, or mortgagee, or other person dealing in good faith, will not be concerned or entitled to question whether the real estate is required for purposes of administration so as to justify a sale or other dealing by the personal representatives, unless their powers are determined by assent or conveyance to the devisee or heir, or unless more than twenty years have elapsed since the death of the testator or intestate (*o*); indeed, it is doubtful whether the effect of the first clause of this sub-section is not to render applicable to a sale of real estate by executors or administrators the rule laid down as to sales of leaseholds and other personal estate, viz., that no lapse of time, even exceeding twenty years, puts an end to the power of an executor to deal with the assets so as to entitle purchasers, etc., to inquire as to the necessity for the sale or other dealing with the estate (*p*).

But though this rule would apply to dealings with real estate as between executors or administrators and *bonâ fide* purchasers, and others dealing with them, the effect of the proviso at the end of the sub-section appears to be to give the devisee or heir a right to require that recourse shall not be had to the real estate for purposes of administration except if and so far as the personalty primarily applicable for those purposes proves to be insufficient; and in the event of an executor or administrator applying the real estate out of due course, it is conceived that the devisee or heir might obtain an injunction to restrain such application or claim damages therefor.

Saving of right of devisee or heir to prevent unnecessary sales, etc.

(*o*) *Re Tanqueray-Willaume and Landau*, 20 Ch. D. 465.

(*p*) *Re Whistler*, 35 Ch. D. 561; *Re Venn & Furze's Contract*, [1894] 2 Ch. 101.

2. Payment of Legacies out of Real Estate.

Question whether the Act of 1897 renders real estate liable to payment of legacies.

It is to be observed that the proviso only qualifies the substantive enactment contained in the first clause of this sub-section so far as relates to the order of application of real and personal assets respectively, and the liability of real estate to be charged with legacies. By sub-section (2) of this section (*q*) all rules of law relating to the liabilities of personal representatives in respect of personal estate are to apply to real estate, so far as the same are applicable; by the first clause of sub-section (3), real estate is to be administered with the same "incidents" as personal estate; and by section 4 (*r*) the personal representatives may, in the absence of any contrary provision in a will, with the consent of a person entitled to a legacy, appropriate any part of the residuary estate to satisfy the legacy.

Reasons for thinking real estate is so liable.

Now, liability to payment of legacies after the debts are paid is a settled and well-known incident of personal estate, and it would hardly seem that the Act of 1897 would have empowered personal representatives to appropriate real estate to payment of legacies, unless it was intended that the real estate should be liable to such payments. It would, therefore, seem that the result of this Act is to render the real estate of a testator liable to payment of legacies as if the testator had by his will charged the legacies thereon, but so that by virtue of the proviso at the end of section 2, sub-section (3), the recourse must not be had to the real estate for the payment of legacies except and so far as the personal estate is primarily insufficient for the purposes of such payments; and that a testator may, if he thinks fit, charge his real estate with payment of legacies either *pari passu* with or in exoneration of his personal estate. If, however, such was, as on the whole it

(*q*) *Ante*, p. 60. (*r*) *Post*, p. 112.

would appear to have been, the intention of the Legislature, it is perhaps to be wondered at that so important a change in the law should not have been clearly and positively enacted, instead of leaving such intention to be inferred from incidental and somewhat ambiguous expressions scattered throughout different sections of the Act.

It will be well that testators should insert provisions in their wills, giving clear directions as to whether their legacies are to be paid in case the personal estate should be insufficient, and, if so, as to how far, and in what proportion, the real estate is to be liable to such payments. *Advisability of providing by will as to payment of legacies out of real estate.*

3. ORDER OF APPLICATION OF ASSETS IN ADMINISTRATION.

The Land Transfer Act, 1897, expressly retains in force the rules of law hitherto in force as to the order of the application of assets in the administration of the estate of a testator or intestate. *Saving of existing order of application.*

Section 2, sub-section (3) of the Act provides that nothing therein contained shall alter or affect the order in which real or personal assets respectively are now applicable in or towards the payment of funeral and testamentary expenses, debts, or legacies.

The order in which the assets of a deceased person are applied in administration is as follows (*s*) :— *Statement of the rule.*

(1.) The general personal estate.
(2.) Real estate devised or directed to be sold to pay debts.

(*s*) See Seton (4th ed.), 989, 990 ; Theobald on Wills (14th ed.), pp. 656—664 ; Jarman on Wills (5th ed.), Vol. II. pp. 1430—1432. In the last-named treatise the order of administration of items 4 and 5 is transposed in deference to the decision of KAY, J. in *Re Bate*, 43 Ch. D. 600 ; but this decision has not been followed in

(3.) Real estate not charged with debts, which, but for the recent statute, would descend to the heir.

(4.) Real estate charged with debts and devised subject to such a charge.

(5.) General pecuniary legacies rateably.

(6.) Real estate devised either specifically or as residue, and personal estate specifically bequeathed rateably.

(7.) Real and personal property appointed by will in exercise of a general power of appointment.

---

4. Effect of the Act on the Distinction between Legal and Equitable Assets.

A change in the law of considerable importance to the creditors of a deceased person has been effected by the Act of 1897 in regard to the administration of assets.

Distinction between legal and equitable assets.

Legal assets have been defined (*t*) to be such as come into the hands and power of an executor or administrator, or such as he is entrusted with by law *virtute officii* to dispose of in the course of administration. Equitable assets, on the other hand, are those assets the right to which, or to recover which, vests in the executor otherwise than *virtute officii* (*u*).

Distinction refers to remedy, not nature of estate.

It may be observed that the distinction between legal and equitable assets in no way depends upon the legal or equitable nature of the property forming the assets (*x*),

---

later cases by STIRLING, J. in *Re Stokes*, 67 L. T. 223, by KEKEWICH, J. in *Re Butler*, [1894] 3 Ch. 250, and by CHITTY, J. in *Re Salt*, [1895] 2 Ch. 203; so that the balance of authority seems in favour of the order of administration as stated in the text.

(*t*) Story on Equity, Ch. IX. s. 551. See Williams on Executors, p. 1548, Williams on Real Assets (9th ed.), Vol. II., pp. 5, 6.

(*u*) *Cook* v. *Gregson*, 3 Drew. 547, 550.

(*x*) *Ibid*, at p. 549.

nor does the fact of the assets being recoverable by the executor only by invoking the equitable jurisdiction of the court necessarily involve the conclusion that the assets so recovered will be equitable assets; the distinction refers to the remedy of the creditor. Thus, in the case of an equity of redemption of leaseholds, the equity of redemption being personalty, and so vesting in the executor *virtute officii* is legal assets, although the subject-matter is equitable, and although the right to redeem is enforceable at the instance of the executor only by virtue of the exercise by the court of its equitable jurisdiction (*y*). In such a case the executor is liable at law to a creditor seeking payment out of such assets.

Hitherto the chance of creditors, having preferential rights of payment otherwise than by reason of specialty (*z*), obtaining any final advantage over the general body of creditors, must have been determined by the nature and extent of the assets distributable. From early times the assets for payment of debts in the hands of a personal representative have been divided into two classes, viz., "legal" and "equitable" assets. It is in respect of the former alone that any right of preference in payment of debts has been acknowledged, or, notwithstanding the Acts 32 & 33 Vict. c. 46 and 38 & 39 Vict. c. 77, s. 10, exists (*a*) in the case of those creditors of a deceased person who have no specific charge upon the assets, the latter class of assets having always been distributable *pari passu* upon the principle that equality is equity (*b*). Moreover, the right to

Rules as to proof in the case of real and equitable assets respectively.

(*y*) *Ibid*, at p. 551.
(*z*) *E.g.* judgment creditors; see as to preferential rights of particular creditors, Williams on Executors (9th ed.), Vol. I., pp. 852 *et seq*. Where an estate is insolvent, specialty and simple contract creditors are now paid *pari passu*, see *ante*, p. 98.

(*a*) *Re William's Estate*, L. R. 15 Eq. 270; *Re Stubb's Estate*, 8 Ch. D. 154; *Smith* v. *Morgan*, 5 C. P. D. E. 337; *Re Maggi*, 20 Ch. D. 545; *Re Leng*, [1895] 1 Ch. 652.
(*b*) *Wilson* v. *Fielding*, 2 Vern. 763.

CHAP. VII.

preferential payment out of legal assets has been considerably circumscribed by the rule as to hotchpot laid down by courts of equity, by which no creditor whose debt has been partially satisfied out of legal assets in priority to other creditors having no right to preferential payment, is allowed to prove for the balance of his debt, in competition with the other creditors, against equitable assets, unless he first brings into hotchpot the amount preferentially received by him (c). It is thus a matter of extreme importance to a creditor having a preferential right to payment, that there should be sufficient legal assets in the hands of the representative of a deceased person to satisfy his debt in full.

Effect of charge of debts, etc., under former law.

In regard to realty in connection with the question of assets, which is the matter now specially under consideration, where realty was devised to executors for the payment of debts, or where executors were given a mere power of sale over realty devised to another, it was for some time considered that the proceeds of the sale of the realty became legal assets in the hands of the executors (d). Lands devised to other persons than the executors, charged with the payment of debts, or in trust to pay debts, were always considered in the nature of trust property to be administered by a court of equity, and not to belong to the executor by virtue of his office. Such lands were therefore called equitable assets, and were from the first distributable *pari passu* according to equitable principles. Later, it was decided that the mere circumstance of the devise being to the persons who were also executors did not affect the nature of the assets, whether the devise was to the executors and their heirs or to the executors simply; and that a power given to the executors to sell

(c) *Bain v. Sadler*, L. R. 12 Eq. 570.

(d) See Williams on Real Assets p. 2.

did not prevent the proceeds of sale from becoming equitable assets (*e*).

Chap. VII.

The principle upon which the court acted in determining that these classes of real assets which had formerly been considered legal were in future to be considered equitable, and distributable as such, was that these assets were not the property of the personal representative *virtute officii* (*f*), and could not be rendered such by any devise or other direction of the testator (*g*).

Principle on which it was held that real estate charged with debts was equitable assets.

By parity of reasoning it would appear that all real property vesting under the Act of 1897 in the executor or administrator for distribution by him as personal representative in payment of debts so far as necessary, must be treated as legal assets notwithstanding any devise in trust to pay debts, or charge for the payment of debts, contained in the will.

Same principle appears now to render real estate, whether charged or not, legal assets.

The result appears to be that the class of assets called legal asset has impliedly been considerably enlarged by the present Act; that it has been enlarged indeed to such an extent as to render for the future any right to preferential payment out of legal assets which a creditor may be able to maintain, a real and substantial advantage in almost every case of administration.

Result as affecting claims to preferential payment.

The order of priority of payment of debts by the personal representative of a deceased person may be shortly stated as follows :—

(1.) Funeral expenses (*h*).
(2.) Testamentary expenses including the costs of probate or taking out administration (*i*), and

---

(*e*) *Serin* v. *Okeley*, 2 Atk. 50 ; *Vik* v. *Prime*, 1 Bro. C. C. 138 ; *Bailey* v. *Ekins*, 7 Ves. 319 ; *Clay* v. *Willis*, 1 B. & C. 364 ; *Barker* v. *May*, 9 B. & C. 489.

(*f*) *Cook* v. *Greyson*, 3 Drew. 547.
(*g*) *Barker* v. *May*, 9 B. & C. 489, 494.
(*h*) *Rex* v. *Wade*, 1 Pri. 627.
(*i*) 2 Blackst. Comm. 511.

also all expenses incident to the proper performance of the duty of an executor (*k*). The costs of an administrative action are testamentary expenses (*l*).

(3.) Debts due to the Crown (*m*).

(4.) Debts to which special priority is given by particular statutes, such as debts due to the parish by its overseers (*n*), to paving commissioners by their treasurers and collectors (*o*), to friendly societies by their officers, and regimental debts of officers and soldiers (*p*).

(5.) Judgments in courts of record whether prior in point of time or not (*q*).

(6.) Recognizances and statutes (*r*).

(7.) Debts by specialty.

(8.) Simple contract debts.

But the priority of specialty debts over simple contract debts is now abolished (*s*).

(*k*) *Sharp* v. *Lush*, 10 Ch. D. 468.
(*l*) *Penny* v. *Penny*, 11 Ch. D. 440.
(*m*) Wentw. Off. Ex. 261. See *Littleton* v. *Hibbins*, Cro. Eliz. 793.
(*n*) 17 Geo. 2, c. 38, s. 3.
(*o*) 57 Geo. 3, c. 29, s. 51.
(*p*) 38 & 39 Vict. c. 60, s. 15
(*q*) Wentw. Off. Ex. 270.
(*r*) 2 Blackst. Comm. 341.
(*s*) 32 & 33 Vict. c. 46.

CHAPTER VIII.

TRANSFER TO DEVISEE OR HEIR.

1. Assent to Devises.

THE object of the provisions now under consideration of the Land Transfer Act, 1897, being to facilitate the administration of the estates of deceased persons, such object is necessarily attained when the administration is completed. Accordingly, section 3 of the Act provides that on completion of an administration, the real estate of the deceased testator or intestate shall be transferred to and enjoyed by the devisee or heir-at-law, subject, and without prejudice, to any dealings therewith by the personal representatives for purposes of administration, but otherwise apparently in like manner as such devisee or heir-at-law would, but for this Act, have been entitled to take and enjoy the property directly upon the decease of the testator or intestate. *Ultimate rights of devisees and heirs to unapplied realty.*

This section enacts as follows:—

(1.)—At any time after the death of the owner of any land, his personal representatives may assent to any devise contained in his will, or may convey the land to any person entitled thereto as heir, devisee, or otherwise, and may make the assent or conveyance, either subject to a charge for the payment of any money which the personal representatives are liable to pay, or without any such charge; and on such assent or conveyance, subject to a charge for all moneys (if any) which the personal representatives are liable to pay, all liabilities of the personal representatives in respect of the land shall cease, except as to any acts done or contracts entered into by them before such assent or conveyance. *Provision for transfer to heir or devisee.*

CHAP. VIII.

Assent or conveyance necessary to vest real estate in devisee or heir.

Inasmuch as by section 1 of the Act real estate on death vests in the personal representatives of the deceased, notwithstanding any contrary disposition in his will, it follows that nothing vests in the devisee by a devise, nor to the heir-at-law under an intestacy, without the express or implied assent of the real representatives or a conveyance by them to him of the property. A like rule has always prevailed with regard to personalty (*t*).

Accordingly, it would seem that until assent to a devise, the devisee will not be a necessary party to an action respecting the real estate devised (*u*).

Inchoate right before assent or conveyance.

Until assent, however, the devisee will have an inchoate right to the property devised, which will be capable of conveyance *inter vivos* by the devisee, and in case of his death before assent, will apparently devolve on his personal representatives as part of his real estate (*x*).

Relation back of assent.

The assent of the real representatives will relate back to the death of the testator, and so confirm any intermediate dealings with the property by the devisee (*y*).

The doctrine of assent has not hitherto extended to a devise of an estate in fee, nor to any estate carved out of the fee by the testator's will; so, where an owner in fee devised the same in fee, in tail or for life, the devisee might have entered without the assent of the executors.

By section 3, sub-section (1), the representatives are empowered either to assent to a devise or to convey the land devised to the person entitled thereto.

(*t*) *Lampet's case*, 10 Rep. 52b; *Bolles* v. *Nyseham*, Dyer, 254b; *Northey* v. *Northey*, 2 Atk. 77; see Co. Litt. 111a; Wentw. Off. Ex. 69.

(*u*) See *Const* v. *Harris*, Turn. & R. 514.

(*x*) Wentw. Off. Ex. 69.

(*y*) *Saunder's case*, 5 Rep. 12b; Wentw. Off. Ex. 69, 445, 446; Toller, 311.

In the case of personalty, no question of assent arises under an intestacy, there being no specific or pecuniary legacies; but the administrator, after discharging the liabilities of the intestate, distributes the residue of the assets amongst the next-of-kin, which may be done either by payment of money, delivery of chattels, transfers of stock, etc., or assignment of leaseholds to the persons entitled, to answer whose shares such properties have been respectively appropriated.

So, in the case of an intestacy of real estate, a conveyance from the representatives should be taken by the heir-at-law, so as to effectually vest the property in the latter.

Where, however, real estate is devised, it would seem that the assent of real representatives to the devise will effectually pass the property to the devisee without the necessity for any conveyance. It will, however, be generally advisable for a devisee, no less than an heir, to take a conveyance so as to obviate any question as to whether the personal representatives really assented to the devise.

After the real representatives have given their assent or conveyed the property, it is conceived that the legal title to the property will vest in the devisee or heir-at-law, as has hitherto been, and is still the rule with regard to a term of years bequeathed on any specific legacy (z); and, accordingly, that the devisee or heir-at-law will be entitled to maintain an action against any persons, including the personal representatives, to recover possession of the property (a).

Action for recovery of possession after assent.

It has been held that if after an assent to a bequest of a term of years, the property is sold by the legatee

---

(z) *Adams* v. *Pierce*, 3 P. Wms. 209; *Williams* v. *Atkins*, 223; 12. *Doe* v. *Guy*, 3 East. 120. See *Cole*
(a) *Bastard* v. *Stukeley*, 2 Lev. v. *Miles*, 10 Hare, 179.

CHAP. VIII. to a *bonâ fide* purchaser, it will no longer be liable in the hands of the purchaser to the claims of creditors of the testator (*b*).

Assent to devise of particular estate is assent to remainders and vice versâ.

If a testator devises real estate in strict settlement, or to several persons by way of remainders, the assent of the real representatives to the entry on the property of the first tenant for life will be deemed to be impliedly an assent to the devise as regards the estates in remainder. And, conversely, their assent to the devise of any one estate in remainder will entitle the first tenant for life to enter on the land, and enure to the benefit of all other persons entitled in remainder for the several estates of the devisees, constituting the whole but one estate. So, where a testator bequeathed the clear rental of a leasehold house to his wife for life, and after her decease to his son, and after his decease to his children equally, with remainders over in default of issue, the executors proved the will and paid the rents to the widow during her life, and after her death to the son during his life, it was held that the assent of the executors to the life estates was an assent to the estates in remainder (*c*).

Assent to gifts of residue.

The doctrine of assent applies not only to specific bequests, but also to gifts of residue, and an executor may assent to part of a residuary gift, without assenting to the whole (*d*).

Assent to devise is assent to annexed condition.

An assent to a bequest or devise is an assent to a condition, or a contingency annexed to the devise. So, where a term of years was bequeathed to an executor for his life, he paying to A. the sum of 50*l.*, with remainder to B., payment by the executor of the 50*l.*

(*b*) *Chamberlain* v. *Chamberlain*, 1 Ch. Ca. 257.

(*c*) *Stevenson* v. *Mayor of Liverpool*, L. R. 10 Q. B. 81. See *Adams* v. *Pierce*, 3 P. Wms. 12;

Com. Dig. "Administration," Ch. 6, Wentw. Off. Ex. 426.

(*d*) *Austin* v. *Beddoe*, 41 W. R. 619.

to A. will be a sufficient assent to the devise of the remainder to B (*e*).

Where, however, a personal representative enters on land, he must have been taken to have entered as such, and not as devisee, unless there be other evidence of his assent to the devise; and the rule is the same whether the devisee is sole real representative or one of several such representatives. If, therefore, the representative having entered on the land, does only acts which are equally applicable or inapplicable to his title as devisee as to his character as representative, he will be presumed to have acted only in his character of representative. But if his dealings with the property are inconsistent with the duty of a real representative, his assent to the devise will be presumed (*f*).

Entry by personal representative on land not proof of assent to devise to him.

So, where a life interest in furniture was given to an executrix, her taking possession of the goods was held to be no assent to the gift in remainder (*g*).

Where there are several personal representatives, the assent of one or more to a bequest of personalty is sufficient (*h*); but inasmuch as an assent to a devise obviously operates as a transfer of real estate, it seems clear that the concurrence of all the personal representatives will be necessary unless the sanction of the court to an assent by one or some only of them is obtained (*i*). On the death of one of them, the power to give assent to a devise will, as it is conceived, devolve on the survivors or survivor, in like manner as it does with respect to a bequest of personalty (*k*).

Assent of one representative sufficient.

(*e*) *Young* v. *Holmes*, 1 Str. 70.
(*f*) *Doe* v. *Sturgess*, 7 Taunt. 217.
(*g*) *Richards* v. *Brown*, 22 L. J. Ch. 1082. See further as to what acts of an executor will or will not be deemed to amount to an assent to his own legacy, Williams on Executors (9th ed.), Vol. II., pp. 1233—1239, and cases there cited.

(*h*) *Holkirk* v. *Holkirk*, 4 Madd. 51; *Worthington* v. *Evans*, 1 S. & St. 165; *Cole* v. *Miles*, 10 Hare, 179.
(*i*) See s. 2 (2) of the Act of 1897, set out *ante*, p. 60.
(*k*) *Flanders* v. *Clark*, 3 Atk. 510.

Chap. VIII.

If land be devised to one of several real representatives, he may assent to the devise without the assent or concurrence of the other real representatives and retain the land accordingly (*l*); and it would seem that he may give such assent before probate of the will or grant of administration (*m*).

Assent by married woman executrix.

It is clear that a personal representative who is a married woman may assent to a devise without the concurrence of her husband, inasmuch as by the Married Women's Property Act, 1882, she is rendered capable of entering into any contract, including the acceptance of the office of an executrix or administratrix (*n*); and it has been held that the concurrence of the husband is not necessary in the administration bond on grant to his wife of letters of administration (*o*).

Infant cannot assent.

A real representative who is an infant cannot, of course, assent to a devise until he attains full age; but his administrators *durante minore ætate* may assent on his behalf (*p*).

Assent before probate.

It would seem that an executor may assent to a devise before probate (*q*); and that the death of a personal representative in the meantime will not affect the validity of such assent, although until probate or grant of letters of administration *cum testamento annexo*, the will is not admissible as evidence (*r*).

It has sometimes been thought that, inasmuch as an executor may assent before probate, the vendor of lands which he has acquired by testamentary disposition can make a good title without probate, and that the purchaser

---

(*l*) *Townson* v. *Tickell*, 3 B. & Ald. 40.
(*m*) Perkins, s. 572.
(*n*) 45 & 46 Vict. c. 75, ss. 1, 24.
(*o*) *Re Ayres*, 8 P. D. 168.
(*p*) *Prince's case*, 5 Rep. 29 b.; *Anon.*, 1 Freem. 288.

(*q*) *Ante*, p. 62.
(*r*) *R.* v. *Stone*, 6 T. R. 298; *Pinney* v. *Pinney*, 3 B. & Cr. 335; *Brazier* v. *Hudson*, 8 Sim. 67; *Fenton* v. *Clegg*, 9 Exch. 680.

ASSENT TO DEVISES.

is not entitled to require the will to be proved (s), but it is submitted that such a proposition cannot be sustained.

Chap. VIII.

Unless the will is proved there will be a defect in the title of the devisee which may prove inconvenient when he desires to deal with the property. The assent or conveyance will be good so far as it goes for purposes of title, but there will be no legal evidence that the person purporting to give the assent or to make the conveyance had any power to do so (t). As soon as the probate has been obtained, this defect in evidence will be supplied, and the claim of title will be perfected accordingly.

Probate necessary to complete title.

The will may be proved at any time, even after the death of the executor; and, on this being done, a previous assent or conveyance will be admissible in evidence, so that the devisee will be enabled to make a good title to a purchaser or mortgagee, by deducing the same from the deceased owner through his personal representatives (u).

The above remarks do not, however, seem to apply to a conveyance to the heir by an administrator before a grant of administration, which would apparently be ineffectual (v).

Conveyance before grant of administration.

A personal representative ought not to assent to a devise until he is satisfied that the assets of the testator are sufficient to pay the debts of the testator in full without rendering the devisee liable to restore the property devised, wholly or in part, for the purpose of satisfying the claims of creditors (x).

Liability of executor assenting before debts are fully paid.

In such a case, the creditors may either sue the real representative personally for *devastavit*, and recover

---

(s) See Dyer, 367 a.
(t) Cru. Dig. 264, 532.
(u) Prest. Abstr. Vol. III. p. 146. And see cases cited *supra*, note (r).

(v) See *ante*, pp. 62, 63.
(x) *Duke of Devon* v. *Atkins*, 3 P. Wms. 383. See Shep. Touchst. 455.

from him the value of the property, to the devise of which he has prematurely assented (*y*); or they may follow the assets into the hands of the devisee into whose possession they have come, however such property may have been changed or altered, and all profits or increments thereof, so long as the property claimed as assets is capable of being identified as in fact acquired with or shown to represent the original assets (*z*).

Assent is irrevocable.

But an assent once given is irrevocable, and will prevent the real representative from recovering possession of the land from the devisee, unless a deficiency in the assets is subsequently created by the discovery of liabilities of the testator which were unknown at the time when the assent was given (*a*); or unless the assent was given under a misapprehension (*b*).

Assent must be absolute and unconditional.

An assent must be absolute and not clogged with any condition subsequent; though it would seem that a representative may agree to give his assent upon the performance of a condition precedent. If an assent is given on the terms that the devisee shall thereafter do or abstain from any act, the condition will be rejected, and the assent will be deemed to have been given absolutely (*c*). And it would seem that if an assent were to be given upon condition that the same should be void unless the devisee should do or abstain from a specified act, and if upon default the representative should obtain a reconveyance from the devisee, such reconveyance would be liable to be set aside (*d*).

(*y*) *Spon* v. *Smith*, 3 Russ. 511.
(*z*) *Marsh* v. *Russell*, 3 My. & Cr. 31; see *Pennell* v *Deffell*, 4 De G. M. & G. 372; *Re Hallett*, 13 Ch. D. 696.
(*a*) *Davis* v. *Davis*, 8 Vin. Abr. 423, pl. 35; *Noel* v. *Robinson*, 2 Ventr. 358; *Orr* v. *Kaimes*, 2 Ves. 194; *Coppin* v. *Coppin*, 2 P. Wms. 296.

(*b*) *Livesey* v. *Livesey*, 3 Russ. 287. See Wentw. Off. Ex. 415; *Mead* v. *Lord Ossery*, 3 Atk. 238.
(*c*) Wentw. Off. Ex. 429.
(*d*) *Westwick* v. *Wyers*, 4 Rep. 28 b.; see Com. Dig. "Administration," c. 8.

In the absence of any conveyance or formal declaration, the assent of real representatives to a devise may be expressly given by parol or by writing however informal, or may be implied from any expression or act on their part which clearly indicates their concurrence in or agreement to the taking of the property by the devisee.

Implication of assent from informal expressions.

Very slight and informal expressions, if sufficiently clear to indicate intention, have been construed as assents to the taking of legacies, as for instance the following: "I intend you to have your legacy according to the devise" (*e*); "The legacy is ready for you whenever you will call for it (*f*).

Where an executor allowed the legatee of a term to receive the rents and profits, his assent to the bequest might be implied (*g*); so also, where the executor for several years paid the rent of leaseholds and charged the legatee with the payment in account (*h*); and where the executor applied the rents of leaseholds for the maintenance of the legatee during minority in accordance with a proviso in that behalf contained in the will, he was held to have assented to the bequest of the corpus (*i*).

Implication from acts of executors.

An obvious result of the provisions of the Act of 1897, in vesting the real estate of a deceased person in his real representatives until they assent to a devise thereof or convey the property devised to the devisee, is to render it necessary, on any subsequent dealing with such property by the devisee, for a purchaser or mortgagee to require satisfactory evidence that the real

Purchasers etc., entitled to evidence of assent.

(*e*) See *Doe* v. *Tatchell*, 3 B. & Ad. 675; *Barnard* v. *Pomfret*, 5 My. & Cr. 70; see also Com. Dig. "Administration," c. 6.
(*f*) *Hawker* v. *Saunders*, Cowp. 293: see *Barnard* v. *Pomfret*, *supra*.
(*g*) Wentw. Off. Ex. 414.
(*h*) *Doe* v. *Maberley*, 6 C. & P. 126.
(*i*) *Passmore* v. *Yardley*, Plowd. 539.

representatives of the testator have assented to the devise. In general, unless there is a conveyance to the devisee or an instrument expressly declaring assent to the devise, the real representatives should be required to testify their assent by concurring in the purchase deed or mortgage, and to confirm the same (*k*).

It will therefore generally be advisable in practice for a devisee or heir to obtain from the real representatives of his testator or ancestor a conveyance to him of the real estate, or at all events a formal instrument expressly declaring assent to his taking the property.

No particular form of assent necessary.

Assent is only a perfecting act, for it is the will of the testator which gives the estate or interest to the devisee or legatee, and therefore generally the law does not prescribe any particular form in which an assent must be given (*l*). And the Act of 1897 does not prescribe any form, except for the purpose of obtaining registration (*m*), or even require an assent to a devise to be in writing.

Presumption of assent after lapse of time.

A title depending upon a conveyance by a devisee at a remote period may, no doubt, be safely accepted by a purchaser without requiring strict evidence of the assent of the personal representatives to the devise; for, in transactions which have happened at a remote date, the rule obtains that "*ex diuturnitate temporis omnia praesumuntur solemniter esse facta*" (*n*); and, accordingly, it would be presumed that the real representatives had done that which it was their duty to do (*o*).

So also if a devisee entered into possession and retains the same for several years without interruption, it

---

(*k*) Prest. Abstr., Vol. III., p. 145.

(*l*) Byth. & Jarm. Conv. Vol. I., p. 176.

(*m*) See s. 3 (3) of the Act. This prescribed form is given in the schedule to the recently issued Provisional Land Transfer Rules (Form 15). See *post* Appendix.

(*n*) Co. Litt. 6 a.; 2 Inst. 118, 302.

(*o*) Williams, Executors (9th ed.), Vol. II., p. 1230.

would be presumed, in the absence of evidence to the contrary, that the personal representatives had assented to the devise (*p*). And after the death of an executor, after the debts are paid, his assent may be presumed (*q*).

But where a legatee of leaseholds entered into possession without any express assent of the executors, and shortly afterwards quitted possession, it was left to the jury to say whether there was sufficient evidence of assent, and whether a contract by the legatee to grant an underlease was to be presumed to have been entered into by him as owner of the term of years, or as agent of the executors (*r*).

It would seem that the question whether or not there is sufficient evidence of assent, in the absence of any express and clear declaration of assent, is one of fact for the jury to determine, even though it depends on the lawful and somewhat critical comparison of the terms of a deed with other circumstances and facts of the case (*s*).

Assent or no assent is question for jury.

---

2. Right of Devisees and Heirs to Compel Conveyance.

After the funeral and testamentary expenses and debts of the testator have been fully paid, and a sufficient fund has, if necessary, been set apart to meet contingent liabilities, the next duty of an executor is to pay the legacies and distribute the residue among the persons entitled thereto (*t*). And a specific legatee or his assignee or representatives can thereupon compel

Rule as to rights of legatees.

(*p*) Prest. Abstr., Vol. III., p. 145. See *Cole* v. *Miles*, 10 Hare, 179.
(*q*) *Cray* v. *Willis*, 2 P. Wms. 531.

(*r*) *Richardson* v. *Gifford*, 1 Ad. & Ell. 52; 3 Nev. & M. 325.
(*s*) Per Alderson, B., in *Mason* v. *Farnell*, 12 M. & W. at p. 682.
(*t*) Williams, Executors (9th ed.), Vol. II., pp. 897 *et seq.*

CHAP. VIII. the executor to give his assent if he refuse to do so without just cause (*u*).

This principle is applied to real estate, the right to recover which, subject to requirements for purposes of administration, is given to a devisee or heir, by section 3 of the Act of 1897, which enacts as follows :—

Jurisdiction of court to order conveyances.

(2.) At any time after the expiration of one year from the death of the owner of any land, if his personal representatives have failed on the request of the person entitled to the land to convey the land to that person, the court may, if it thinks fit, on the application of that person, and after notice to the personal representatives, order that the conveyance be made, or, in the case of registered land, that the person so entitled be registered as proprietor of the land, either solely or jointly with the personal representatives.

Liability of representatives refusing to convey.

It has been seen that this Act expressly declares that the personal representatives of a deceased owner of land are to be deemed to be trustees for the persons entitled (*x*). It is a well settled rule with regard to trustees, that, when they have no longer any active duty to perform because their trust has been fully performed, it is their duty to convey or transfer the trust property to the persons beneficially entitled thereto or as they direct, and if they refuse to do so without good reason they will be liable to pay the costs of an action to compel conveyance or transfer (*y*).

Where an action to compel assent or conveyance is brought against a personal representative, the indorsement must show that he is being sued in a representative capacity (*z*).

(*u*) Com. Dig. "Administration," c. 8.
(*x*) *Ante*, p. 52.
(*y*) *Payne* v. *Barker*, Bridg. 24; *Jones* v. *Lewis*, 1 Cox 199; *Willis* v. *Hiscox*, 4 My. & Cr. 197; *Hampshire* v. *Bradley*, 2 Coll. 34.
(*z*) R. S. C., Order IV. r. 4; App. A., Part III., s. 7.

If the beneficiary has conveyed real estate to which he is entitled subject to the requirements of administration, before assent of the personal representatives or conveyance of the property by them to him, then, upon completion of the administration, the purchaser from the beneficiary will be entitled to call upon the personal representatives to convey to him the legal estate, and a refusal to do so may render them liable to costs (a). It would seem that the purchaser may bring an action in such a case to compel a conveyance by the real representatives without making the beneficiary vendor a party (b).

<small>CHAP. VIII.

Right of purchasers from devisee or heir before assent or conveyance.</small>

A married woman beneficially entitled to her separate use, and not restrained from anticipation, may compel the personal representatives to convey to herself or her husband (c).

<small>Married woman.</small>

Of course the personal representative will be entitled to refuse to assent to a devise or to convey the property if he can show that retention of the property is necessary to enable him to provide for the discharge of debts or liabilities of the deceased which are of course paramount to the claims of the devisee or heir (d).

<small>Grounds on which personal representatives may refuse to convey.</small>

A personal representative, like a trustee, may also refuse to assent or convey if, upon the face of the will, the title of the claimant is doubtful (e); and the fact that in refusing, they have acted under the advice of counsel, even though mistaken, may induce the court to absolve them from payment of costs (f).

(a) *Angier* v. *Stannard*, 3 My. & K. 566.

(b) *Goodson* v. *Ellison*, 2 Russ. 583; *Holford* v. *Phipps*, 3 Beav. 434; 4 Beav. 475.

(c) *Thirby* v. *Yeats*, 1 Y. & C.C.C. 438. The restraint only applies during coverture. See *Buttonshaw* v. *Martin*, Johns. 89.

(d) *Chaffe* v. *Kelland*, 1 Roll. Abr. 929, tit. Executors (A), pl. 1; *Elwell* v. *Quash*, 1 Stra. 20. See Wentw. Off. Ex. 212.

(e) *Angier* v. *Stannard*, 3 My. & K. 566; see *Darey* v. *Thornton*, 9 Hare, 232; *Re Cull*, L. R. 20 Eq. 561.

(f) *Stott* v. *Milne*, 25 Ch. D. 710.

CHAPTER IX.

Appropriation of Real Estate to Legacies, etc.

By section 4 of the Act of 1897 it is enacted that :—

Appropriation of land in satisfaction of legacy or share in estate.

(1.) The personal representatives of a deceased person may, in the absence of any express provision to the contrary contained in the will of such deceased person, with the consent of the person entitled to any legacy given by the deceased person or to a share in his residuary estate, or, if the person entitled is a lunatic or an infant, with the consent of his committee, trustee, or guardian, appropriate any part of the residuary estate of the deceased in or towards satisfaction of that legacy or share, and may for that purpose value in accordance with the prescribed provisions the whole or any part of the property of the deceased person in such manner as they think fit. Provided that before any such appropriation is effectual, notice of such intended appropriation shall be given to all persons interested in the residuary estate, any of whom may thereupon within the prescribed time apply to the court, and such valuation and appropriation shall be conclusive save as otherwise directed by the court.

Extent of this enactment

It would at first sight be inferred from the marginal note to this section that its provisions relate solely or mainly to appropriation of land, but the expressions "land" or "real estate" do not occur in the section, which is of general application, including all the residuary estate of a deceased person, whether real or personal.

APPROPRIATION OF REAL ESTATE. 113

With regard to legacies payable *in futuro*, by way of annuity (*g*), or given contingently upon the happening of a specified event, the rule has been that the executors are not merely justified, but compellable in equity to set apart a sufficient part of the testator's personal estate to answer the legacy as and when it becomes due and payable (*h*); but the rule was different where the legacy was to be raised out of real estate (*i*). And in some cases where there is no risk of loss to the fund, the court instead of ordering appropriation of part of personalty to answer contingent legacy has ordered the whole residue to be paid over to the residuary legatee upon his giving satisfactory security to pay the legacy if the contingency should occur (*k*).

<small>Former rule as to legacies *in futuro*.</small>

As regards immediate legacies it has been generally considered in practice, where the will contains no express powers of appropriation, that the safest course to adopt is for the executors to sell, call in and convert into money such parts of the personal estate of the testator as do not consist of money, and to pay over the legacies to the persons entitled thereto in cash, so as to avoid any disputes in the future as to the propriety of the appropriation. And, accordingly, express powers are often given by will to the executors or trustees either with or without the consent of such beneficiaries as are of full age to appropriate property in or towards satisfaction of legacies or shares of residue (*l*).

Now, however, in the case of any testator dying on or after January 1st, 1898, it would seem that personal

<small>Effect of the Act.</small>

(*g*) An annuity is a legacy; see *Sibley* v. *Perry*, 7 Ves. 522; *Bromley* v. *Wright*, 7 Hare, 334; *Ward* v. *Grey*, 26 Beav. 485; *Gaskin* v. *Rogers*, L.R. 6 Eq. 284.
(*h*) *Phipps* v. *Annesley*, 2 Atk. 273; *Johnson* v. *Mills*, 1 Ves. Sen. 282; *Green* v. *Pigott*, 1 Bro. C. C. 103; *Pullen* v. *Smith*, 5 Ves. 21.

(*i*) *Gawler* v. *Standerwick*, 2 Cox, 15.
(*k*) See *Webber* v. *Webber*, 1 S. & St. 311. See *Re Braithwaite*, 21 Ch. D. 121.
(*l*) Byth. & Jarm. Conv., 4th ed., Vol. VII., p. 881; Key & Elph. Conv., Vol. II., p. 700, 821.

representatives will have full power to appropriate any part of the residuary estate of a deceased person, whether real or personal, in or towards satisfaction of legacies given by his will or shares of residue, provided that no direction to the contrary is contained in the will, that the prescribed consents are obtained, and that no person interested in the residuary estate after due notice of the intended appropriation objects thereto (*m*).

The question as to whether this enactment does or does not alter the law as to the ultimate devolution, on completion of the administration, of real estate on an intestacy has already been considered (*n*).

Duties of personal representative after appropriation.

Where a legacy is given *in futuro* and the executors appropriate any part of the testator's residuary estate to answer the same, they become trustees of the part so appropriated, with all the duties and liabilities of ordinary trustees (*o*). They are therefore bound to make and continue authorized investments of the appropriated fund and would not be justified in lending that fund with other parts of the residuary estate so as to render it undistinguishable from other parts of the estate, as, for instance, by lending it on a contributory mortgage (*p*), but it would seem that an appropriation by personal representatives of part of the real or personal estates to answer more than one legacy or share of residue would be valid (*q*).

Appropriation once duly made is absolute.

On the other hand, if an appropriation of residuary estate has once been made with the consent of the persons entitled to a legacy or share of a residue, or if by the terms of the will, the executors being

---

(*m*) See *ante*, p. 112.
(*n*) *Ante*, p. 84.
(*o*) *Byrchall* v. *Bradford*, 6 Madd. 240; *Phillips* v. *Munnings*, 2 My. & Cr. 309; *Ex parte Dover*, 5 Sim. 500.

(*p*) *Webb* v. *Jones*, 29 Ch. D. 660; see *Massingberd's Settlement*, 63 L. T. 296.
(*q*) See *Re Walker*, 62 L. T. 449.

authorized to appropriate without consent *bonâ fide* exercise their discretion to the best of their judgment, the beneficiaries must take the appropriated fund, subject to any subsequent variations in value whether by way of increment (*r*), or loss (*s*); provided that the appropriation was of an investment subsisting at the time of the testator's death, or authorized by law on the terms of his will (*t*).

Where part of residuary estate of a deceased person is appropriated to answer a contingent legacy, the tenant for life is entitled to the income of a fund until the happening of the contingency.

<small>Right of tenant for life pending a contingency.</small>

A form of appropriation of land in satisfaction of a legacy or share in residuary estate is given in the schedule to the Provisional Land Transfer Rules recently issued (*u*). This form is, however, merely intended for production to the registrar, with other prescribed evidence of appropriation of land, to enable the person to whom the land is appropriated to be registered as proprietor of that land in place of the deceased proprietor (*x*). The appropriation in the prescribed form does not of itself operate as a conveyance of the land, and, except as regards registered land, a formal deed of conveyance will be required.

<small>Instrument of appropriation.</small>

(*r*) *Green* v. *Pigott*, 1 Bro. C. C. 105; *Burgess* v. *Robinson*, 3 Mer. 9. See *Rock* v. *Hardman*, 6 Madd. 254; *Kimberley* v. *Tew*, 4 Dr. & War. 139. But see *contra*, *Sitwell* v. *Bernhard*, 6 Ves. 543.

(*s*) *Frazer* v. *Murdock*, 6 App. Cas. 855 at p. 864. See *Kendall* v. *Russell*, 3 Sim. 424.

(*t*) *Re Waters*, W. N. (1889), 39.

(*u*) See Form 16, Appendix, *post*, p. 150.

(*x*) Rule 15, Appendix, *post*, p. 150.

CHAPTER X.

MISCELLANEOUS MATTERS.

1. Registration of Proprietorship of Real Estate.

The enactments contained in Part I. of the Act of 1897 with regard to registration of devisees and heirs under the Land Transfer Act, 1875 (*u*), as amended by this Act, are as follows:—

Provisions in Act of 1897, Part I., as to registration.

By section 3, sub-section (1), after the expiration of a year from the death of any owner of land, the court may, in lieu of ordering a conveyance to the devisee or heir, order "in the case of registered land that the person so entitled be registered as proprietor of the land either solely or jointly with the personal representatives."

And the same section further enacts as follows:—

(3.) Where the personal representatives of a deceased person are registered as proprietors of land on his death, a fee shall not be chargeable on any transfer of the land by them unless the transfer is for valuable consideration.

(4.) The production of an assent in the prescribed form (*v*) by the personal representatives of a deceased proprietor of registered land shall authorize the registrar to register the person named in the assent as proprietor of the land.

(*u*) 38 & 39 Vict. c. 87.
(*v*) For the prescribed form of assent, see Form 15 in Appendix, *post*, p. 150.

And by section 4 of the same Act, after empowering personal representatives to appropriate real estate to satisfy legacies and shares of residue, it is enacted that—

> (3.) In the case of registered land, the production of the prescribed evidence of an appropriation under this section shall authorize the registrar to register the person to whom the property is appropriated as proprietor of the land.

The expression "prescribed" means in the Land Transfer Act, 1875 (*w*), and in this Act, prescribed by any general rules made in pursuance of these Acts (*x*).

Meaning of "prescribed."

General Rules, under section 111 of the Land Transfer Act, 1875, and section 2 of the Act of 1897, were issued on December 29th, 1897, intituled "Provisional Land Transfer Rules, 1897," and will be found set out in the Appendix to these notes.

General rules.

Transmissions of land on the death of a registered proprietor thereof are dealt with in rules 14 to 19 inclusive. They provide that on production of probate or letters of administration of a registered proprietor of land his executors or administrators shall be entitled to registration as such of the land in his place. They prescribe the evidence on production of which a person claiming under an assent or appropriation shall be entitled to be registered as proprietor of the land in the place of the deceased proprietor. They further provide, where a settlement is created by will, for the registration of all proper restrictions and inhibitions; and they relieve the registrar from all obligation to inquire into the terms of the will, the probate or copy or

---

(*w*) 38 & 39 Vict. c. 87, see s. 4 of that Act.

(*x*) 38 & 39 Vict. c. 87, s. 111; 60 & 61 Vict. c. 65, s. 22 (2).

Compulsory registration in county of London.

abstract of which may, if the parties desire it, be left with the registrar for safe custody.

By a notice recently issued under section 20 of the Act of 1897 by the Office of Land Registry of a draft order, it appears that as respects the county of London on and after July 1st, 1898, it is proposed that registration of title to land is to be compulsory on sale.

2. STAMP DUTIES.

Assent.

An assent to a devise, if given by deed, will require a stamp of 10s., as a deed not otherwise charged (y). But a deed is not generally necessary for the purpose of giving an assent, nor is an assent under the Act of 1897 required to be under seal or even in writing, except for the purpose of obtaining registration (z); if the assent is given under hand only, it will not require any stamp.

Conveyance to devisee or heir.

A deed of conveyance by personal representatives to a devisee or heir will require a stamp of 10s.

Conveyance on appropriation.

By section 4 of the Act of 1897, after empowering personal representatives to appropriate any residuary estate to satisfy legacies or shares of residue (a), it is enacted that—

> (2.) Where any property is so appropriated a conveyance thereof by the personal representatives to the person to whom it is appropriated shall not, by reason only that the property so conveyed is accepted by the person to whom it is conveyed in or towards the satisfaction of a legacy or a share in residuary estate, be liable to any higher stamp duty than that payable on a transfer of personal property for a like purpose.

(y) 54 & 55 Vict. c. 39, Sched. (a) Ante, p. 112.
(z) Ante, p. 108.

3. LIABILITY TO SUCCESSION AND ESTATE DUTY.

With regard to liability to duty, the Act of 1897 enacts as follows:—

> Section 5. Nothing in this part of this Act shall affect any duty payable in respect of real estate or impose on real estate any other duty than is now payable in respect thereof.

By section 42 of the Succession Duty Act, 1853 (*b*), succession duty is to be a first charge on the interest of the successor, and of all persons claiming in his right, in all the real property in respect whereof such duty shall be assessed; and by the Customs and Inland Revenue Act, 1889 (*c*), the liability attaches as against a purchaser for valuable consideration or mortgagee till the expiration of six years from the date of the notice to the commissioners of the succession, or of the first payment of any instalment or part of the duty, or till after two years from the payment of the last instalment or part, or in any other case for twelve years after the happening of the event giving rise to the claim to duty. It will not, therefore, be safe for a purchaser or mortgagee to take a conveyance from the personal representatives of a deceased owner of land without ascertaining that succession duty has been paid or provided for.

Succession duty.

The same precaution should be taken by a purchaser or mortgagee as regards estate duty, unless the sale or mortgage is for the purpose of raising the duty. By section 9 of the Finance Act, 1894 (*d*), it is enacted as follows:—

Estate duty.

> (1.) A rateable part of the estate duty on an estate in proportion to the value of any property which does not pass to the executor as such, shall be a first charge

---

(*b*) 16 & 17 Vict. c. 51. (*d*) 57 & 58 Vict. c. 30.
(*c*) 52 & 53 Vict. c. 7.

on the property in respect of which duty is leviable; provided that the property shall not be so chargeable as against a bona fide purchaser thereof for valuable consideration without notice.

* * * * *

(5.) A person authorized or required to pay the estate duty in respect of any property shall, for the purpose of paying the duty or raising the amount of the duty when already paid, have power, whether the property is or is not vested in him, to raise the amount of such duty and any interest and expenses properly paid or incurred by him in respect thereof by the sale or mortgage of or a terminable charge on that property or any part thereof.

APPENDIX.

LAND TRANSFER ACT, 1897.
(60 & 61 Vict. Cap. 65.)

An Act to establish a Real Representative, and to amend the Land Transfer Act, 1875. [6th August, 1897.]

WHEREAS it is expedient to establish a real representative, and to amend the Land Transfer Act, 1875, in this Act referred to as "the principal Act:"   38 & 39 Vict. c. 87.

Be it therefore enacted by the Queen's most Excellent Majesty, by and with the advice and consent of the Lords Spiritual and Temporal, and Commons, in this present Parliament assembled, and by the authority of the same, as follows:—

Part I.
Establishment of a Real Representative.

1.—(1.) Where real estate is vested in any person without a right in any other person to take by survivorship it shall, on his death, notwithstanding any testamentary disposition, devolve to and become vested in his personal representatives or representative from time to time as if it were a chattel real vesting in them or him.   *Devolution of legal interest in real estate on death.*

(2.) This section shall apply to any real estate over which a person executes by will a general power of appointment, as if it were real estate vested in him.

(3.) Probate and letters of administration may be granted in respect of real estate only, although there is no personal estate.

(4.) The expression "real estate," in this part of this Act, shall not be deemed to include land of copyhold tenure or customary freehold in any case in which an admission or any act by the lord of the manor is necessary to perfect the title of a purchaser from the customary tenant.

(5.) This section applies only in cases of death after the commencement of this Act.

2.—(1.) Subject to the powers, rights, duties, and liabilities hereinafter mentioned, the personal representatives of a deceased person shall hold the real estate as trustees for the persons by law beneficially entitled thereto, and those persons shall have the same power of requiring a transfer of real estate as persons beneficially entitled to personal estate have of requiring a transfer of such personal estate.   *Provisions as to administration.*

APPENDIX.

(2.) All enactments and rules of law relating to the effect of probate or letters of administration as respects chattels real, and as respects the dealing with chattels real before probate or administration, and as respects the payment of costs of administration and other matters in relation to the administration of personal estate, and the powers, rights, duties, and liabilities of personal representatives in respect of personal estate, shall apply to real estate so far as the same are applicable, as if that real estate were a chattel real vesting in them or him, save that it shall not be lawful for some or one only of several joint personal representatives, without the authority of the court, to sell or transfer real estate.

(3.) In the administration of the assets of a person dying after the commencement of this Act, his real estate shall be administered in the same manner, subject to the same liabilities for debt, costs, and expenses, and with the same incidents, as if it were personal estate; provided that nothing herein contained shall alter or affect the order in which real and personal assets respectively are now applicable in or towards the payment of funeral and testamentary expenses, debts, or legacies, or the liability of real estate to be charged with the payment of legacies.

(4.) Where a person dies possessed of real estate, the court shall, in granting letters of administration, have regard to the rights and interests of persons interested in his real estate, and his heir-at-law, if not one of the next-of-kin, shall be equally entitled to the grant with the next-of-kin, and provision shall be made by rules of court for adapting the procedure and practice in the grant of letters of administration to the case of real estate.

Provision for transfer to heir or devisee.

3.—(1.) At any time after the death of the owner of any land, his personal representatives may assent to any devise contained in his will, or may convey the land to any person entitled thereto as heir, devisee, or otherwise, and may make the assent or conveyance, either subject to a charge for the payment of any money which the personal representatives are liable to pay, or without any such charge: and on such assent or conveyance, subject to a charge for all moneys (if any) which the personal representatives are liable to pay, all liabilities of the personal representatives in respect of the land shall cease, except as to any acts done or contracts entered into by them before such assent or conveyance.

(2.) At any time after the expiration of one year from the death of the owner of any land, if his personal representatives have failed on the request of the person entitled to the land to convey the land to that person, the court may, if it thinks fit, on the application of that person, and after notice to the personal representatives, order that the conveyance be made, or, in the case of registered land, that the person so entitled be registered as proprietor of the land, either solely or jointly with the personal representatives.

(3.) Where the personal representatives of a deceased person are registered as proprietors of land on his death, a fee shall not be chargeable on any transfer of the land by them unless the transfer is for valuable consideration.

(4.) The production of an assent in the prescribed form by the personal representatives of a deceased proprietor of registered land shall authorize the registrar to register the person named in the assent as proprietor of the land.

4.—(1.) The personal representatives of a deceased person may, in the absence of any express provision to the contrary contained in the will of such deceased person, with the consent of the person entitled to any legacy given by the deceased person or to a share in his residuary estate, or, if the person entitled is a lunatic or an infant, with the consent of his committee, trustee, or guardian, appropriate any part of the residuary estate of the deceased in or towards satisfaction of that legacy or share, and may for that purpose value in accordance with the prescribed provisions the whole or any part of the property of the deceased person in such manner as they think fit. Provided that before any such appropriation is effectual, notice of such intended appropriation shall be given to all persons interested in the residuary estate, any of whom may thereupon within the prescribed time apply to the court, and such valuation and appropriation shall be conclusive save as otherwise directed by the court. *Appropriation of land in satisfaction of legacy or share in estate.*

(2.) Where any property is so appropriated a conveyance thereof by the personal representatives to the person to whom it is appropriated shall not, by reason only that the property so conveyed is accepted by the person to whom it is conveyed in or towards the satisfaction of a legacy or a share in residuary estate, be liable to any higher stamp duty than that payable on a transfer of personal property for a like purpose.

(3.) In the case of registered land, the production of the prescribed evidence of an appropriation under this section shall authorize the registrar to register the person to whom the property is appropriated as proprietor of the land.

5. Nothing in this part of this Act shall affect any duty payable in respect of real estate or impose on real estate any other duty than is now payable in respect thereof. *Liability for duty.*

Part II.

Amendments of the Land Transfer Act, 1875.

6.—(1.) Settled land may (at the option of the tenant for life) be registered either in the name of the tenant for life, or, where *Settled land.*

there are trustees with powers of sale, in the names of those trustees, or, where there is an overriding power of appointment of the fee simple, in the names of the persons in whom that power is vested.

(2.) There shall also be entered on the register such restrictions or inhibitions as may be prescribed, or may be expedient, for the protection of the rights of the persons beneficially interested in the land.

(3.) Where land already registered is assured to the uses of a settlement, the instrument of transfer may be in a specially prescribed form, which shall operate as a conveyance to the uses of the settlement, and it shall be the duty of the trustees of the settlement (if any) to concur in the instrument, and to apply for the entry on the register of the proper restrictions or inhibitions under this section. If there are no such trustees, the registrar shall inquire into the terms of the settlement, and shall enter on the register such restrictions or inhibitions as may be prescribed, or as appear to him to be in accordance with this section.

(4.) On the death of a tenant for life, registered as proprietor of settled land, it shall be the duty of the trustees of the settlement (if any) to apply for the registration of his successor or successors, with such restrictions or inhibitions (if any) as may be in accordance with this section. If the trustees neglect to apply or if there are no such trustees, the registrar shall proceed under the forty-first section of the principal Act in such manner as may be prescribed.

(5.) Where a settlement is created by the will of, or otherwise arises in consequence of the death of, a sole registered proprietor of land or of an undivided share in land, it shall be the duty of his personal representatives to apply for the registration of the person entitled to be registered as proprietor, and for the entry on the register of proper restrictions or inhibitions in accordance with this section.

(6.) The settlement, or an abstract or copy thereof, may be filed in the registry for reference in the prescribed manner, but such filing shall not affect a purchaser or mortgagee for value from the registered proprietor with notice of its provisions, or entitle him to call for production of the settlement, or for any information or evidence as to its contents.

(7.) The registered proprietor of settled land and all other necessary parties (if any) shall, on the request, and at the expense, of any person entitled to an estate, interest, or charge conveyed or created for securing money actually raised at the date of such request, charge the land in the prescribed manner with the payment of the money so raised.

(8.) Subject to the maintenance of the right of the registered proprietor to deal by registered disposition, or by way of mortgage by deposit, with any land whereof he is registered as proprietor, the estates, rights, and interests of the persons for the time being entitled under any settlement comprising the land shall be unaffected by the registration of that proprietor.

(9.) A person in a fiduciary position may apply for, or concur in, or assent to, any registration authorized by this section, and, if he is a registered proprietor, may execute an instrument of transfer or charge in the prescribed form in favour of any person whose registration is so authorized.

(10.) In this section the expressions "tenant for life," "settled land," "settlement," and "trustees of the settlement," have the same meaning as in the Settled Land Acts, 1882 to 1890.

7.—(1.) Where any error or omission is made in the register, or where any entry in the register is made or procured by or in pursuance of fraud or mistake, and the error, omission, or entry is not capable of rectification under the principal Act, any person suffering loss thereby shall be entitled to be indemnified in the manner in this Act provided. {Right to indemnity in certain cases. 38 & 39 Vict. c. 87.}

(2.) Provided that where a registered disposition would if unregistered be absolutely void, or where the effect of such error, omission, or entry, would be to deprive a person of land of which he is in possession, or in receipt of the rents and profits, the register shall be rectified and the person suffering loss by the rectification shall be entitled to the indemnity.

(3.) A person shall not be entitled to indemnity for any loss where he has caused or substantially contributed to the loss by his act, neglect, or default, and the omission to register a sufficient caution, notice, inhibition, or other restriction to protect a mortgage by deposit or other equitable interest, or any estate or interest created under section forty-nine of the principal Act, shall be deemed neglect within the meaning of this sub-section.

(4.) Where the register is rectified under the principal Act by reason of fraud or mistake which has occurred in a registered disposition for valuable consideration, and which the grantee was not aware of and could not by the exercise of reasonable care have discovered, the person suffering loss by the rectification shall likewise be entitled to indemnity under this section.

(5.) The registrar may, if the applicant desires it, and subject to an appeal to the court, determine whether a right to indemnity has arisen under this section, and, if so, award indemnity. In the event of an appeal to the court, the applicant shall not be required to pay any costs except his own, even if unsuccessful, unless the court shall consider that the appeal is unreasonable.

(6.) Where indemnity is paid for a loss, the registrar, on behalf of the Crown, shall be entitled to recover the amount paid from

Appendix.

21 Jac. 1. c. 16.

any person who has caused or substantially contributed to the loss by his act, neglect, or default.

(7.) A claim for indemnity under this section shall be deemed a simple contract debt, and for the purposes of the Limitation Act, 1623, the cause of action shall be deemed to arise at the time when the claimant knows, or but for his own default might know, of the existence of his claim. This section shall apply to the Crown in like manner as it applies to a private person.

Land certificates, office copies of registered leases, and certificates of charge.

8.—(1.) So long as a land certificate, office copy of a registered lease, or certificate of charge, is outstanding, it shall be produced to the registrar on every entry in the register of a disposition by the registered proprietor of the land or charge to which it relates, and on every registered transmission or rectification of the register, and a note of every such entry, transmission, or rectification shall be officially endorsed on the certificate or office copy, and the registrar shall have the same powers of compelling the production of certificates and office copies as are conferred on him by sections one hundred and nine and one hundred and ten of the principal Act as to the production of maps, surveys, books, and other documents.

(2.) Where a land certificate or office copy of a registered lease has been issued, the vendor shall deliver it to the purchaser on completion of the purchase, or, if only a part of the land comprised in the certificate or office copy is sold, he shall, at his own expense, produce, or procure the production of, the certificate or office copy in accordance with this section for the completion of the purchaser's registration. Where the certificate or office copy has been lost or destroyed, the vendor shall pay the costs of the proceedings required to enable the registrar to proceed without it.

(3.) A new land certificate, office copy of a registered lease or certificate of charge, shall not be granted by the registrar in place of a former certificate, or office copy, which has been lost or destroyed, unless the applicant has filed with the registrar a statutory declaration and such other evidence, if any, as the registrar may think necessary, stating the fact and circumstances of the loss or destruction of the former certificate or office copy, nor until at least one advertisement of the application in the London Gazette and three advertisements in a London daily morning newspaper shall have been published at intervals of not less than seven days, and three advertisements in a local newspaper circulating in the district in which the land is situate, and such indemnity (if any) given as the registrar shall think fit.

(4.) Where a transfer of land is made by the registered proprietor of a charge, in exercise of the power of sale conferred by the charge, it may be registered, and a new land certificate may be issued to the purchaser, without production of the former land certificate, but the certificate of charge (if any) must be produced or accounted for in accordance with this section. Subject to any stipulation to the contrary the proprietor of a registered charge shall not be entitled to have custody of the Land Certificate, or to require a Land Certificate to be applied for :—

(i.) On the first registration of freehold or leasehold land, and on the registration of a charge, a land certificate, office copy of the registered lease, or certificate of charge, as the case may be, shall be prepared, and shall either be delivered to the registered proprietor or deposited in the registry as the said proprietor may prefer;

(ii.) If so deposited in the registry it shall be officially endorsed from time to time, as in this section provided, with notes of all subsequent entries in the register affecting the land or charge to which it relates;

(iii.) The registered proprietor may at any time apply for the delivery of the certificate or office copy to himself or to such person as he may direct, and may at any time again deposit it in the land registry;

(iv.) The preparation, issue, endorsement, and deposit in the registry of the certificate or office copy shall be effected without cost to the proprietor.

The registered proprietor of any freehold or leasehold land or of a charge may, subject to any registered estates, charges, or rights, create a lien on the land or charge by deposit of the land certificate or office copy of registered lease, or certificate of charge; and such lien shall, subject as aforesaid, be equivalent to a lien created by the deposit of title deeds or of a mortgage deed of unregistered land by an owner entitled in fee simple or for the term or interest created by the lease for his own benefit, or by a mortgagee beneficially entitled to the mortgage.

9.—(1.) The provisions of section eight of the Conveyancing and Law of Property Act, 1881, shall apply, so far as applicable thereto, to transfers of registered land as though such transfers were made by deed, and a transfer of land made by the proprietor of a registered charge with power of sale shall operate as a conveyance in professed exercise of the power of sale conferred by the said Act.

Transfers and charges.
44 & 45 Vict c. 41.

(2.) The provisions of sections nineteen, twenty, twenty-one (except sub-sections one and four), twenty two, twenty-three, and twenty-four of the same Act, shall similarly apply to registered charges.

(3.) Every registered proprietor of land may in the prescribed manner charge it with an annuity or other periodical payment, and

APPENDIX.

the provisions of the principal Act and this Act with regard to charges shall apply to any such charge. Every registered proprietor of land may charge it, in favour of a building society under the Building Societies Acts, by means of a mortgage made in pursuance of or consistent with the rules of that society, and the mortgage shall be deemed a charge made in the prescribed manner, and shall be registered accordingly.

(4.) Nothing contained in any charge shall (i) take away from the registered proprietor thereof the power of transferring it by registered disposition or of requiring the cessation thereof to be noted on the register, or (ii) affect any registered dealing with land or a charge in respect of which the charge is not expressly registered or protected, in accordance with the principal Act and this Act.

(5.) The registrar may, on the application, or with the consent, of the registered proprietor of the land, and of the proprietors of all registered charges (if any) of equal or inferior priority, alter the terms of a charge.

(6.) Where a person on whom the right to be registered as proprietor of land or of a charge has devolved by reason of the death or bankruptcy of the registered proprietor, or has been conferred by an instrument of transfer or charge, in accordance with the principal Act and this Act, desires to transfer or charge the land or to deal with the charge before he is himself registered as proprietor, he may do so in the prescribed manner, and subject to the prescribed conditions. Subject to the provisions of the principal Act with regard to registered dealings for valuable consideration, a transfer or charge so made shall have the same effect as if the person making it were registered as proprietor.

Penalty for unqualified persons drawing instruments.

10. Every person who (not being a barrister or a duly certificated solicitor, notary public, conveyancer, special pleader, or draftsman in equity) either directly or indirectly, for or in expectation of any fee, gain, or reward, draws or prepares any instrument of transfer or charge, or an application to register restrictive conditions, or to alter or discharge, or alter the priority of a registered charge, or any other prescribed instrument, shall incur a fine not exceeding fifty pounds, which shall be recoverable before a court of summary jurisdiction in manner provided by the Summary Jurisdiction Acts.

Provided that this section shall not extend to—

(a) any public officer drawing or preparing instruments and applications in the course of his duty ; or
(b) any person employed merely to engross any instrument or application.

As to statute of 32 Hen. 8. c. 9.

11. Section two of the statute of the thirty-second year of the reign of Henry the Eighth, chapter nine, which prohibits sales and

other dispositions of land of which the grantor or his predecessor in title has not been in possession for one whole year previously to the disposition being made, is hereby repealed.

APPENDIX

12. A title to registered land adverse to or in derogation of the title of the registered proprietor shall not be acquired by any length of possession, and the registered proprietor may at any time make an entry or bring an action to recover possession of the land accordingly. Provided that where a person would, but for the provisions of the principal Act or of this section, have obtained a title by possession to registered land, he may apply for an order for rectification of the register under section ninety-five of the principal Act, and on such application the court may, subject to any estates or rights acquired by registration for valuable consideration in pursuance of the principal Act or this Act, order the register to be rectified accordingly. And provided also, that this section shall not prejudice, as against any person registered as first proprietor of land with a possessory title only, any adverse claim in respect of length of possession of any other person who was in possession of such land at the time when the registration of such first proprietor took place.

As to title by possession.

13.—(1.) On every application to register land with an absolute title, or to register a transmission of land, the registrar shall inquire as to Succession Duty and Estate Duty.

(2.) If, on such application, it appears that there is, or is capable of arising, any such liability to Succession Duty or Estate Duty as would affect the purchaser from the person to be registered as proprietor if the land were unregistered, the registrar shall enter notice of the liability on the register in the prescribed manner.

(3.) Succession Duty and Estate Duty shall not—
  (a) unless so noted on the register; or
  (b) unless in the case of a possessory title the liability to the duty was, at the date of the original registration of the land, subsisting or capable of arising; or
  (c) unless in the case of a qualified title the liability to the duty was included in the exceptions made on such original registration of the land;

affect a bonâ fide registered purchaser for full consideration in money or money's worth, although he may have received extraneous notice of the liability in respect thereof.

As to succession and estate duty.

14.—(1.) So much of section eighty-three of the principal Act as prohibits the registration of undivided shares, and limits the number of co-proprietors, and relates to the description, boundaries, and extent, and alteration of the description of registered land is repealed.

Repeal in part of 38 & 39 Vict. c. 87, s. 83.

APPENDIX.

(2.) Registered land shall be described in the prescribed manner by means of the ordnance map, together with such further verbal particulars (if any) as the applicant for registration may desire, and the registrar, or the court, if the applicant prefers, may approve, regard being had to ready identification of parcels, correct description of boundaries, and, as far as may be, uniformity of practice.

Provisions as to land held by incumbents of benefices.

1 & 2 Vict. c. 23.
2 & 3 Vict. c. 49.
51 & 52 Vict. c. 20.

15.—(1.) Where the incumbent of a benefice and his successors are the registered proprietors of land—

(i.) No disposition thereof shall be registered unless a certificate in the prescribed form shall be obtained—

(a) in case of sales under the Parsonages Act, 1838, or the Church Building Act, 1839, or any Acts amending or extending the same respectively, from Queen Anne's Bounty; or

(b) in case of sales under the Glebe Lands Act, 1888, or any Acts amending or extending the same, from the Board of Agriculture; or

(c) in all other cases, from the Ecclesiastical Commissioners.

(ii.) No lien shall be created by deposit of the land certificate,

and an inhibition shall be placed on the register and on the land certificate accordingly.

The production of a certificate from any of the above-mentioned bodies shall be a sufficient authority to the registrar to register the disposition in question, and it shall be the duty of the proper body to grant such certificate in all cases in which the facts admit thereof.

(2.) On the registration of the incumbent of a benefice and his successors as the proprietors of registered land, if it shall be certified by Queen Anne's Bounty, or shall otherwise appear, that such land was originally purchased by Queen Anne's Bounty or was otherwise appropriated or annexed by or with the consent or the concurrence of Queen Anne's Bounty to the benefice for the augmentation thereof, the registrar shall enter a note to that effect on the register.

(3.) Where the incumbent of a benefice is entitled to indemnity under the provisions of this Act, the money shall be paid to Queen Anne's Bounty and appropriated by them to the benefice.

(4.) The term "benefice" in this section shall comprehend all rectories with cure of souls, vicarages, perpetual curacies, donatives, endowed public chapels and parochial chapelries, and chapelries or districts belonging, or reputed to belong, or annexed, or reputed to be annexed, to any church or chapel.

Provisions as to vendor and purchaser on sales.

16.—(1.) A purchaser of registered land shall not require any evidence of title, except—

(i.) the evidence to be obtained from an inspection of the register or of a certified copy of, or extract from, the register:

(ii.) a statutory declaration as to the existence or otherwise of matters which are declared by section eighteen of the principal Act and by this Act not to be incumbrances;

(iii.) if the proprietor of the land is registered with an absolute title, and there are incumbrances entered on the register as subsisting at the first registration of the land, either evidence of the title to those incumbrances, or evidence of their discharge from the register;

(iv.) where the proprietor of the land is registered with a qualified title, the same evidence as above provided in the case of absolute title, and such evidence as to any estate, right, or interest excluded from the effect of the registration as a purchaser would be entitled to if the land were unregistered:

(v.) if the land is registered with a possessory title, such evidence of the title subsisting or capable of arising at the first registration of the land as the purchaser would be entitled to if the land were unregistered.

(2.) Where the vendor of registered land is not himself registered as proprietor of the land or of a charge giving a power of sale over the land, he shall, at the request of the purchaser and at his own expense, and notwithstanding any stipulation to the contrary, either procure the registration of himself as proprietor of the land or of the charge, as the case may be, or procure a transfer from the registered proprietor to the purchaser.

(3.) In the absence of special stipulation, a vendor of land registered with an absolute title shall not be required to enter into any covenant for title, and a vendor of land registered with a possessory or qualified title shall only be required to covenant against estates and interests excluded from the effect of registration, and the implied covenants under section seven of the Conveyancing and Law of Property Act, 1881, shall be construed accordingly.

17.—(1.) The registered proprietor of land not situated in a district where the registration of title is compulsory, may, with the consent of the other persons (if any) for the time being appearing by the register to be interested therein, and on delivering up the land certificate or office copy of the registered lease and certificates of charge (if any), remove the land from the register.

(2.) After land is removed from the register no further entries shall be made respecting it, and inspection of the register may be made and office copies of the entries therein may be issued, subject to such regulations as may be prescribed.

(3.) If the land so removed from the register is situate within the jurisdiction of the Middlesex or Yorkshire registries named in

APPENDIX.

38 & 39 Vict. c. 87.
Minor amendments in Schedule I.

Registration of small holdings.
55 & 56 Vict. c. 31.

section one hundred and twenty-seven of the principal Act, it shall again be subject to such jurisdiction as from the date of the removal.

18. The principal Act shall be further amended in regard to its minor details in the manner set forth in the First Schedule hereto.

19.—(1.) Where a county council apply in pursuance of section ten of the Small Holdings Act, 1892, for registration as proprietors of land, they may be registered as proprietors of that land, with any such title as is authorized by the principal Act.

(2.) Where a county council, after having been so registered, transfer any such land to a purchaser of a small holding, the purchaser shall be registered as proprietor of the land with an absolute title, subject only to such incumbrances as may be created under the Small Holdings Act, 1892, and in any such case the remedy of any person claiming by title paramount to the county council in respect either of title or incumbrances shall be in damages only, and such damages shall be recoverable against the county council.

PART III.

Compulsory Registration and Insurance Fund.

Power to require registration of title on sale.

38 & 39 Vict. c. 87.

20.—(1.) Her Majesty the Queen may, by Order in Council, declare, as respects any county or part of a county mentioned or defined in the Order, that, on and after a day specified in the Order, registration of title to land is to be compulsory on sale, and thereupon a person shall not, under any conveyance on sale executed on or after the day so specified, acquire the legal estate in any freehold land in that county, or part of a county, unless or until he is registered as proprietor of the land.

(2.) In this section the expression "conveyance on sale" means an instrument executed on sale by virtue whereof there is conferred or completed a title under which an application for registration as first proprietor of land may be made under the principal Act.

(3.) The title with which a proprietor of freehold land is registered in pursuance of this section shall be not less than a possessory title; but nothing in this section shall prevent any person from being registered with any other title if the registrar is satisfied of his title.

(4.) It shall be lawful for Her Majesty in Council to revoke or vary any Order made under this section.

(5.) In the case of every Order proposed to be made under this section, notice shall, six months before the Order is made, be given to the council of the county to which such Order is proposed to be applied. A draft of the proposed Order, together with the name of at least one place within or conveniently near to the county where a district registry office will be established, shall accompany the notice, and shall also be published in the Gazette.

(6.) If within three months after receipt of the draft the county council, at a meeting specially called for the purpose, at which two-thirds of the whole number of the members shall be present, resolve, and communicate to the Privy Council their resolution, that in their opinion compulsory registration of title would not be desirable in their county, the Order shall not be made.

(7.) The first Order made under this section shall not affect more than one county.

(8.) Except as to a county or part of a county which shall have signified through the county council of such county, pursuant to a resolution of such council passed at a meeting at which two-thirds of the whole number of the members shall be present, its desire that registration of title shall be compulsorily applied to it, no further Order shall be made under this section, and in any case no further Order shall be made under this section until the expiration of three years from the making of the first order Provided that in the case of an Order made under this sub-section the provisions of sub-section (6) shall not apply.

(9.) Every Order of Council made under this section shall, within thirty days from the date thereof, if Parliament be then sitting, or within twenty days from the commencement of the next session, if Parliament be not sitting, be laid on the table of both Houses of Parliament, and if within forty days of any order being so laid an Address in either House disapproving of such order be carried, such Order shall be void and of no effect.

(10.) Any Order made under this section shall be made with due regard to the utilisation (if practicable) of any land registry existing in the county to which compulsory registration is proposed to be applied or in any adjoining county.

(11.) For the purposes of this section the word county shall have the same meaning as in the Local Government Act, 1888, and shall include a county borough ; and the word county council shall include the council of such borough. 51 & 52 Vict. c. 11.

(12.)—(i.) In the event of any portion of a county or part of a county as regards which an Order has been made under this section being included in another county or in a county borough as regards which no Order has been made under this section, such Order shall cease to be in force within such included portion of the county.

(ii.) In the event of any portion of a county or part of a county as regards which no Order has been made under this section being included in another county or in a county borough as regards which

APPENDIX.

Insurance fund for providing indemnity

an Order has been made under this section, such Order shall apply to such included portion of the county.

21.—(1.) For the purpose of providing indemnity payable under this Act, there shall be established an insurance fund to be raised by setting apart at the end of each financial year such portion of the receipts from fees taken in the land registry as the Lord Chancellor and the Treasury shall by order determine.

(2.) The insurance fund shall be invested in such names and manner as the Treasury from time to time direct.

(3.) If the insurance fund is at any time insufficient to pay indemnity for any loss chargeable thereon, the deficiency shall be charged on and paid out of the Consolidated Fund of the United Kingdom, or the growing produce thereof; but any sum so paid out of the Consolidated Fund, or the growing produce thereof, shall be repaid out of the money subsequently standing to the credit of the insurance fund.

(4.) Accounts of the fund shall be kept, and be audited as public accounts, in accordance with such regulations as the Treasury from time to time make.

PART IV.

Miscellaneous.

Rules and fee orders.

22.—(1.) Regulations may be made by the Lord Chancellor, under section one hundred and six of the principal Act, altering or adding to the official styles of the registrar and other officers of the registry, for the purposes of this Act.

(2.) General rules under section one hundred and eleven of the principal Act shall be made by the Lord Chancellor with the advice and assistance of the registrar, a judge of the Chancery Division of the High Court to be chosen by the judges of that division, and three other persons, one to be chosen by the General Council of the Bar, one by the Board of Agriculture, and one by the Council of the Incorporated Law Society.

(3.) Orders under section one hundred and twelve and one hundred and twenty-two of the principal Act shall be made by the Lord Chancellor with the advice and assistance of the same persons, and with the concurrence of the Treasury.

(4.) The fee orders relating and incidental to registration of title shall be arranged from time to time so as to produce an annual amount sufficient to discharge the salaries and other expenses (including the annual contribution to the insurance fund) incidental to the working of the principal Act, and this Act, and no more.

38 & 39 Vict. c. 87.

(5.) Subject to any alterations that may be made in accordance with sections one hundred and twelve and one hundred and twenty-two of the principal Act and this section, the fees to be charged in districts where registration of title is compulsory shall, as regards the matters mentioned in the Second Schedule hereto, be as therein set forth.

(6.) Provision may be made by general rules, under section one hundred and eleven of the principal Act, as amended by this Act, for carrying this Act into effect, and in particular for the following purposes:—

- (a.) For carrying out the provisions of this Act with respect to compulsory registration ;
- (b.) For adapting to the registration of proprietors of leasehold land the provisions of the principal Act, as to absolute and possessory titles, and as to land certificates ;
- (c.) For adapting to sub-mortgages and to incumbrances prior to registration the provisions of the principal Act with regard to charges ;
- (d.) For the conduct of official searches against cautions, inhibitions, and such matters of a like nature as may be prescribed, and for enabling the registered proprietor to apply for such searches by telegraph, and for returning the replies in like manner to him or to such other person as he may direct :
- (e.) For enabling cautions to be entered against the registration of possessory and qualified titles as qualified or absolute ;
- (f.) For enabling a mortgagee by deposit to give notice to the registrar by registered letter or otherwise of the deposit with him of the land certificate, office copy of the registered lease, or certificate of charge. Provided that the fee for the entry of any such notice shall not exceed one shilling ;
- (g.) For applying to the grant of leases and dealings with leasehold land the provisions of this Act with respect to compulsory registration ;
- (h.) For allowing the insertion, inserting in the register, and in land certificates, of the price paid or value declared on first registrations, transfers, and transmissions of land ; and
- (i.) For regulating any such matters as are authorised by this Act to be prescribed.

(7.) Provided that nothing in the rules under the said section shall extend to allow the inspection of any entry in the register, except by or under the authority of some person interested in the land or charge to which the entry refers.

(8.) Provision may be made by general orders under section one hundred and eighteen of the principal Act for modifying the provisions of that Act with respect to the formation and

APPENDIX.

Provision for the Yorkshire registries of deeds.

54 & 55 Vict. c. 64.

23.—(1.) At any time after the passing of this Act, and subject to the provisions of section twenty of this Act, the Lord Chancellor may enter into an agreement with the county council of any of the three ridings of Yorkshire for the transfer of the business of the local deed registry established in that riding to the office of land registry.

(2.) The agreement shall be drawn up in accordance with the principles of sections one, three, and four of the Land Registry (Middlesex Deeds) Act, 1891, which provided for the transfer of the Middlesex registry of deeds to the land registry, and shall, after approval by the Treasury, take effect accordingly.

(3.) The whole of the property, assets, and liabilities of the county council, in relation to the local registry, shall be included in the transfer, and shall be taken over by the State at a price to be specified in or ascertained under the terms of the agreement, but no sum shall be payable for compensation in respect of any future loss of fees consequent upon such transfer.

(4.) Unless and until an agreement as aforesaid is concluded the county council may from time to time, at intervals of five years, in the event of their suffering loss, owing to the business of the local registry being diminished by reason of the principal Act and this Act, apply to the Treasury for compensation, and the Treasury shall award such compensation accordingly.

(5.) The compensation shall be made by the payment of a capital sum to the county fund to be determined in case of dispute by arbitration in the usual way on the basis of the receipts and expenditure in respect of the local registry during the three years previous to the claim being made, and that the county fund shall not be placed in a worse financial position by the operation of the Act.

(6.) All payments under this section shall be made out of moneys to be provided by Parliament.

Interpretation.

24.—(1.) All hereditaments, corporeal and incorporeal, shall be deemed land within the meaning of the principal Act and this Act, except that nothing in this Act shall render compulsory the registration of the title to an incorporeal hereditament, or to mines or minerals apart from the surface, or to a lease having less than forty years to run or two lives yet to fall in, or to an undivided share in land, or to freeholds intermixed and indistinguishable from lands of other tenure, or to corporeal hereditaments parcel of a manor, and included in a sale of the manor as such.

(2.) In this Act the expression "personal representative" means an executor or administrator.

25. This Act shall come into operation on the first day of January one thousand eight hundred and ninety-eight.

Commencement of Act.

26. This Act may be cited as the Land Transfer Act, 1897, and shall be construed as one with the principal Act, and that Act and this Act may be cited together as the Land Transfer Acts, 1875 and 1897.

Short title and construction.

SCHEDULES.

THE FIRST SCHEDULE.

Section 18.

MINOR AMENDMENTS OF THE PRINCIPAL ACT.

The sections of the principal Act mentioned in the first column of this Schedule are repealed or amended to the extent and in the manner set forth in the third column.

1. Section in Principal Act.	2. Subject Matter.	3. Extent of Repeal or Nature of Amendment.
2	Only land of freehold tenure to be registered.	If, at any time, land is found to have been registered with absolute or qualified title contrary to the provisions of this section, the registration shall not be annulled, but shall be deemed an error not capable of rectification under the principal Act, and any person suffering loss thereby shall be indemnified accordingly.
11	Registration of leasehold land.	A sub-lease shall, and a term created for mortgage purposes shall not, be deemed a lease within the meaning of this section.
18	Various rights and liabilities not to be incumbrances.	This section shall include estate duty, liability to repair the chancel of any church, liability in respect of embankments, sea and river walls, and drainage rights, customary rights, public rights, and profits à prendre, and, subject to the provisions of this Act, rights acquired or in course of being acquired under the Limitation Acts.
18 (4) (5)	Rights to and in respect of mines and minerals not to be incumbrances.	These sub-sections shall apply only to rights created previously to the registration of the land or the commencement of this Act.
18, last paragraph.	Power for registrar to note on the register the existence of liabilities mentioned in the section.	The power conferred on the registrar shall be exercised in all cases where the abstract of title on first registration or on registration as qualified or absolute discloses the existence of any such liabilities as are mentioned in sub-sections (4) and (5). Where an easement is registered as an incumbrance, the dominant and servient tenements shall be defined, if practicable and required by the parties. Notice of a power of re-entry and of a right of reverter may be entered on the register under this paragraph.

APPENDIX.

1. Section in Principal Act.	2. Subject Matter.	3. Extent of Repeal or Nature of Amendment
19 and 28, second paragraph.	Discharge of incumbrances created prior to the registration of the land, and of registered charges.	These sections shall apply to part discharges.
21	No acquisition of title by adverse possession.	Repealed.
22	Creation of charges	Charges created under this section are subject to the provisions of the principal Act in respect of qualified or possessory titles.
30—33 and 35—38	Effect of transfers of freehold and leasehold land.	In the absence of anything to the contrary in the register, or in the transfer, or (in the case of leasehold land) in the lease, the word "land" in these sections includes the mines and minerals if parcel thereof.
40	Transfer of charges	A registered transferee for value of a charge, and his successors in title, shall not be affected by any irregularity or invalidity in the original charge itself, of which the transferee was not aware when it was transferred to him.
43	Transmission on bankruptcy.	This section shall not apply until it is certified in the prescribed manner by the court having jurisdiction in bankruptcy that the land or charge is part of the property of the bankrupt divisible amongst his creditors. The official receiver shall be entitled to be registered pending the appointment of a trustee.
44, 45, 83 (4)	As to married women	These sections shall not apply to the case of any woman married on or after January 1st, 1883, or to any property to which a married woman is entitled for her separate use.
49	General powers of disposition over land.	This section includes power to sever the mines and minerals from the surface.
50	Notice of leases	The words "made subsequently to the last transfer of the land on the register" are repealed.
58	Registration of restrictions.	The words "for his own sake, or at the request of some person beneficially interested in such land" are repealed, and the section shall apply to charges as well as to land.
66	Notices to the Board of Trade and others on registration of foreshore.	This section shall not apply to registration with a possessory title.
72	Title deeds to be marked with notice of registration.	In the case of registration with a possessory title, the registrar may act on such reasonable evidence as may be prescribed as to the sufficiency of the documents produced, and as to dispensing with their production in special circumstances.

APPENDIX.

1. Section in Principal Act.	2. Subject Matter.	3. Extent of Repeal or Nature of Amendment.
78	Loss or destruction of land certificate.	Repealed.
81	Effect of deposit of land certificate.	Repealed.
82, first paragraph.	Registration of advowsons and other incorporeal hereditaments.	The words "enjoyed in gross" are repealed.
83 (1)	Notices of trusts	Repealed, and the following sub-section substituted:—Neither the registrar nor any person dealing with registered land or a charge shall be affected with notice of a trust, express, implied, or constructive; and references to trusts shall, as far as possible, be excluded from the register.
83 (2)	Undivided shares and joint proprietors.	Repealed.
83 (3)	Entry of no survivorship of joint proprietors.	The words "with their consent" are repealed, and the following words and further provision are added to this sub-section:—"or of the registrar, after "inquiry into title, subject to an appeal "to the court." "Subject to general rules, wherever registered land or a charge is to be entered in the names of two or more joint proprietors, the registrar shall make such entry under this sub-section as may be prescribed, unless it is shown to his satisfaction that the joint proprietors are entitled for their own benefit."
83 (5 and 6)	Description boundaries and extent of registered land.	Repealed.
84	Annexation of conditions to land.	Conditions may be annexed to land at any time, and the section shall apply to any restrictive condition capable of affecting assigns by way of notice.
126	Transfer of titles from the 1862 register.	The words "nevertheless it shall not be "obligatory on any person interested in "an estate registered under the said Land "Registry Act, 1862, to cause such estate "to be registered under this Act" are repealed.
127	Registered land to be exempt from Middlesex and Yorkshire registries.	The section shall not apply to estates and interests excepted from the effect of registration under a possessory or qualified title, or to an unregistered reversion on a registered leasehold title, or to dealings with incumbrances created prior to the registration of the land.

APPENDIX.

Section 22.

THE SECOND SCHEDULE.

The following fees shall be paid in districts where registration of title is compulsory, and shall include all necessary surveying, mapping, and scrivenery, and the preparation, issue, endorsement, or deposit, as the case may be, of a land certificate, office copy, registered lease, or certificate of charge ; discharges of incumbrances, the registration of any necessary cautions, inhibitions or restrictions, the filing of auxiliary documents (if any), and all other necessary costs of and incidental to the completion of each registration or transaction, whether under one or under several titles.

For possessory registration, and for transfers, charges, and transfers of charges for valuable consideration :—

Value.	Fees.
Not exceeding 1,000*l*.	1*s*. 6*d*. for every 25*l*. or part of 25*l*.
Exceeding 1,000*l*. and not exceeding 3,000*l*.	3*l*. for the first 1,000*l*., and 1*s*. for every 25*l*. or part of 25*l*. over 1,000*l*.
Exceeding 3,000*l*. and not exceeding 10,000*l*.	7*l*. for the first 3,000*l*., and 1*s*. for every 50*l*. or part of 50*l*. over 3,000*l*.
Exceeding 10,000*l*.	14*l*. for the first 10,000*l*., and 1*s*. for every 100*l*. or part of 100*l*., up to a maximum of 25*l*. for 32,000*l*.

For transmissions and transfers not for value, notices of leases, and rectification of the register, and land :—

> One quarter of the above fees, according to the capital value of the interest dealt with, with a minimum of 1*s*. and a maximum of 5*l*.

No fees to be charged for inspection of the register.

LAND TRANSFER ACTS, 1875 AND 1897.
PROVISIONAL LAND TRANSFER RULES, 1897.

Interpretation.

1. In these Rules "the Act of 1875" and "the Act of 1897" mean the Land Transfer Acts of those years respectively, and "the Acts" has a corresponding meaning.

First Registration of Settled Land.

2. Application for registration of settled land may be made by any person capable of being registered as proprietor, with the consent of the other persons (if any) whose consent or concurrence is necessary to a sale by that person.

3. In the case of possessory title the proper restriction shall be left with the application, or the Registrar shall be furnished with the information necessary to enable him to draw the proper restriction.

4. In framing restrictions and inhibitions for the protection of settled land, it shall not be the duty of the trustees or of the Registrar to protect the interests of any person who would not have been a necessary party to a sale or mortgage thereof if the land had been unregistered; but it shall be the duty of the trustees, or, if there are no trustees, of the Registrar, to give notice of the restrictions and inhibitions to such of the beneficiaries (if any) as the Registrar shall direct; and any such person can, if he wishes, lodge a caution or apply for an inhibition.

5. The restrictions and inhibitions given in Forms 1 to 5 in the Schedule hereto, shall apply respectively to the various cases in the Schedule set forth.

6. The settlement, whether consisting of one or of several documents, or a copy or abstract thereof, may be left in the Registry for reference and safe custody. It shall not be referred to on the Register, but shall be filed in a separate place under the number of the title to which it relates.

Transfers of Land into Settlement.

7. An instrument of transfer of land to the uses of a settlement may be in one of the Forms 6 to 12 in the Schedule hereto, and shall contain the proper restrictions or inhibitions to be entered on the Register, according to the principles stated in Rule 4 of these Rules. The transfer shall be signed by the tenant for life (if any,

Rule 7 and if of full age), as well as by the transferor and transferee, and all signatures shall be verified.

8. On receipt of an instrument of transfer in such form as aforesaid, the Registrar shall register the transferee named therein as the proprietor of the land, and shall enter on the Register the inhibitions and restrictions contained in the transfer.

9. If it appears to the Registrar that any restriction or inhibition contained in the transfer thus applied for is unreasonable or contrary to the principle on which the Register is kept, or calculated to cause unnecessary inconvenience, he may require the production of the settlement and an abstract or copy thereof, and any further evidence that may be necessary for the purpose of determining, and he shall determine (subject to an appeal to the Court), what restrictions and inhibitions, if any, ought to be registered, and the form thereof.

10. It shall not otherwise be the duty of the Registrar to enquire into the terms of the settlement, but, if the parties desire it, the settlement, or a copy or abstract thereof, may be deposited in the Registry for safe custody and future reference.

11. Where registered land has been brought into settlement, and the existing registered proprietor is the tenant for life under the settlement, and he elects to remain the registered proprietor thereof, it will only be necessary for him to apply for the registration of a restriction and inhibition in Form 1 in the Schedule hereto, or such other restriction or inhibition as may be required, having regard to the terms of the settlement and the Settled Land Acts.

Charges.

12. A charge to secure an annuity may be in Form 13 in the Schedule hereto.

13. An application to alter the terms of a registered charge under section 9 (5) of the Act of 1897 may be in Form 14 in the Schedule hereto, and shall be signed by the registered proprietor of the charge, and by the registered proprietor of the land, and of every charge of equal or inferior priority prejudicially affected by it, and the signatures shall be verified.

Transmissions of Land on Death.

14. On production of the probate or letters of administration of a sole (or sole surviving) registered proprietor of land, dying after 1897, the personal representative named therein shall be registered as proprietor in the place of the deceased proprietor, with the addition of the words, "Executor (or Administrator) of deceased."

15. On production of the probate or letters of administration with will annexed, and of an assent or appropriation in either of the Forms 15 or 16 in the Schedule hereto, or of an instrument of transfer by the personal representative in the usual prescribed Form, and of the probate or letters of administration, the devisee or legatee named in the assent or appropriation or the transferee named in the instrument of transfer shall be registered as proprietor of the land in place of the deceased proprietor. The signatures of the executor or administrator to the assent, appropriation, or transfer shall be verified.

16. Where a settlement is created by the will, or otherwise arises in consequence of the death, of a sole registered proprietor, the personal representative shall, at the proper time, and with the consent of the tenant for life (if of full age) leave in the Registry, together with the probate or letters of administration, a written application for the registration of a proprietor, with the proper restrictions and inhibitions, according to the principles stated in section 6 of the Act of 1897 and Rule 4 of these Rules.

17. On receipt of such an application, the Registrar shall register the proprietor and the inhibitions and restrictions therein named and applied for.

18. If it appears to the Registrar that any restriction or inhibition contained in the application is unreasonable or contrary to the principle on which the Register is kept, or calculated to cause unnecessary inconvenience, he may require the production of the probate (if any) or an abstract or copy thereof, and any further evidence that may be necessary for the purpose of determining, and he shall determine (subject to an appeal to the Court), what restrictions and inhibitions, if any, ought to be registered, and the form thereof.

19. It shall not otherwise be the duty of the Registrar to enquire into the terms of the will, but, if the parties desire it, the probate, or a copy or abstract thereof, may be deposited, in the Registry for safe custody and future reference.

20. Where the trustees of a settlement apply, on the death of a tenant for life, for the registration of a successor under the settlement, they and their solicitor shall make a statutory declaration to the effect that the deceased proprietor was tenant for life, and that they are the trustees of the settlement, and that the person for whose registration they are applying is the successor under the settlement, and that the restrictions and inhibitions (if any) applied for are the proper ones to be entered, or that no restrictions or inhibitions are required. In any case in which the Registrar may deem it desirable that the declaration shall be accompanied by a

RULE 15.

RULE 20. certificate of counsel to the like effect, a certificate to his satisfaction shall be produced.

21. Where such a declaration (and certificate, if required) are produced, the Registrar need not require production of the settlement or any further evidence, but where not produced he shall enquire into the terms of the settlement, and shall satisfy himself that the proper entries are made on the Register.

22. If, on the death of a tenant for life, registered as proprietor of land, the trustees of the settlement neglect to apply for the registration of the new proprietor in his place, or if there are no such trustees, any person interested under the settlement may apply for the registration of a new proprietor. The Registrar shall thereupon enquire into the terms of the settlement, and shall settle draft entries for the Register on the principles stated in section 6 of the Act of 1897 and Rule 4 of these Rules in regard to settled land, and shall give notice thereof to the trustees of the settlement (if any) and to the new tenant for life, and to such other persons (if any) as he may think fit ; and if no valid objection is made thereto shall enter the new proprietor or proprietors accordingly.

Transmissions on Bankruptcy.

23. On production to the Registrar of an order of a Court having jurisdiction in bankruptcy declaring a proprietor a bankrupt, together with a certificate signed by the official receiver that any registered land or charge is part of the property of the bankrupt, divisible amongst his creditors, the official receiver may be registered as proprietor in his place.

24. On production of such an order as last mentioned and of an order appointing a trustee, the trustee may be registered as proprietor.

25. If the official receiver has not been registered as proprietor, the order appointing the trustee, with a certificate signed by the trustee that the land or charge is part of the property of the bankrupt, divisible amongst his creditors, shall be produced to the Registrar.

26. In the liquidation of a company, any resolution or order appointing a liquidator may be filed and referred to on the Register, and, when so registered, shall be deemed to be in force until it is cancelled or superseded on the Register.

Instruments under Section 9 (6) of the Act of 1897.

27. An instrument executed under the 6th sub-section of the 9th section of the Act of 1897 by a person entitled to be registered

as proprietor of land, or of a charge, before he has been registered as such, shall be in the same form as is prescribed for registered dispositions by the registered proprietor.

RULE 27.

28. Such an instrument shall not be registered until the person executing it has been registered as proprietor, or his right to be so registered has been shown to the satisfaction of the Registrar.

29. When such an instrument deals with a portion of the land comprised in a title or with a charge not yet entered on the Register, the form may be varied so far as may be necessary to identify the land or charge dealt with.

Notices as to Death Duties.

30. Where, upon an examination of title made on the first registration of land, the Registrar finds that there is, or may arise, any liability to death duties of the kind mentioned in section 13 of the Act of 1897, he shall enter notice thereof in the Register according to Form 17 in the Schedule hereto.

31. Where, on the death of a registered proprietor of land, his personal representatives are registered as such under Rule 14 of these Rules, notice of liability to duty shall not be entered.

32. If the personal representatives of a deceased proprietor of land assent to a devise or appropriation, or transfer land to any person otherwise than by sale, notice of the liability to duty shall be entered unless there is produced either :

(*a.*) Proof to the satisfaction of the Registrar that all duty payable in respect of the land by reason of the death of the proprietor has been paid or satisfied, or

(*b.*) A certificate from the Commissioners of Inland Revenue in Form 18 in the Schedule hereto, or to that effect, or

(*c.*) Proof to the satisfaction of the Registrar that the applicant is entitled to the land in such a capacity that any liability to duty would not affect a purchaser from him if the land were unregistered.

33. Where a notice of liability to duty has been entered on the Register, it may be cancelled on production of any such evidence as is mentioned in the preceding rule.

Entry of No Survivorship of Joint Proprietors.

34. Where two or more persons apply to be entered as joint proprietors of land or of a charge, notice shall be given them that, by virtue of section 83 of the Act of 1875, as amended by the First Schedule of the Act of 1897, it is intended to make an entry in the Register in Form 19 in the Schedule hereto.

Rule 35.

35. If satisfactory evidence is produced to the Registrar that the proprietors are entitled to the land or charge for their own benefit, or that under the trust upon which they hold the land or charge a sole surviving trustee has power to dispose of the trust property, the entry shall not be made. If such evidence accompanies the application, the notice mentioned in the preceding rule need not be given.

36. An entry in the said Form 19 may at any time be made at the request, or with the consent, of the joint proprietors.

37. When such an entry has been made, and the joint proprietors have been reduced to the number specified in it, the Registrar shall, before registering any disposition by the registered proprietor, require the production of the equitable title to the property, and may give such notices to the persons equitably entitled, or any of them, as he may deem expedient.

Notice of Deposit of Land Certificate.

38. Any person with whom a land certificate, office copy registered lease, or certificate of charge is deposited as security for money may, by writing, give notice to the Registrar of the fact, and on receipt of such notice the Registrar shall enter the same in the Register.

39. So long as a notice of such a deposit is on the Register, no new certificate shall be issued under section 8 (3) of the Act of 1897 without notice to the person with whom the deposit was made.

40. The notice of deposit may be removed on the written request, signed and verified, of the person who placed it on the Register, or his successor in title; or, with his consent in writing, on the like request of the registered proprietor of the land; accompanied in each case by the land certificate.

Forms.

41. The forms in the Schedule hereto shall be adopted so far as practicable, but with such modifications as the parties may desire, and the Registrar approve.

Commencement, Mode of Citation, etc.

42. These Rules shall come into operation on the 1st day of January, 1898, and shall be construed as one with the Land Registry Rules of 1875 and 1889, and may be cited as the Provisional Land Transfer Rules, 1897, and in case of any discrepancy between these Rules and the said Rules of 1875 and 1889, these Rules shall prevail.

Dated the 29th day of December, 1897.

THE SCHEDULE.

Form 1.

Restriction and Inhibition where Tenant for Life is registered as Proprietor, and there are Trustees of the Settlement, and powers of charging for special purposes.

Restriction.—Until further order no transfer of the land is to be made except on sale or exchange, and the purchase moneys on sale are to be paid to *A. B.* of etc., and *C.D.* of etc. [*the trustees of the settlement*], or into court : no sale of the house and land shown and edged red on the plan attached hereto is to be made without the consent of the said *A. B.* and *C. D.* or of the Court, and no charge is to be created without the consent of the said *A. B.* and *C. D.* (*Or, where the tenant for life has power to raise a definite sum for his own use*, if and when the land has been charged to the extent of £   no further charge shall be created without the consent of the said *A. B.* and *C. D.*)

Inhibition.—On the death of *E. F.* of etc. [*the registered proprietor*] no entry is to be made until further order.

Form 2.

Restriction where the Tenant for Life is registered as Proprietor, and has incumbered his beneficial interest, without reserving the right to exercise his statutory powers.

Until further order no transfer or charge shall be registered without the consent of *A. B.* of etc. [*the mortgagee of the life interest*].

Form 3.

Restriction where the Trustees of the Settlement are registered as Proprietors.

Until further order no transfer or charge is to be made without the consent of *A. B.* of etc. [*tenant for life*].

Form 4.

Inhibition where there are no Trustees of the Settlement, and the Tenant for Life is registered as Proprietor.

No transfer is to be made, and no charge is to be created, till further order.

Form 5.

Inhibition where land is settled to such uses as Two Persons, entered as Proprietors, shall jointly appoint, and subject thereto in Settlement.

After the death of either of the joint proprietors no transfer shall be made or charge created till further order.

Form 6.

Instrument of Transfer to give effect to a settlement, under which the existing Registered Proprietor is the Tenant for Life, but the Trustees of the Settlement are to be registered as Proprietors.

LAND REGISTRY.
Land Transfer Acts, 1875 and 1897.

No. of title   .

(*Date.*) In pursuance of the provisions of the settlement dated etc., and made between etc. (*or* created by the will of etc.) under which I,

FORM 6.   *A. B.* of etc. am (*or* have the powers of) tenant for life under the Settled Land Acts, 1882 to 1890, and *C. D.* of etc. and *E. F.* of etc. are the trustees for the purposes of the same Acts, I, the said *A. B.* hereby transfer to the said *C. D.* and *E. F.* all the land comprised in the title above referred to, and apply for the registration of the following restriction (*fill in Form* 3).

FORM 7.

Instrument of Transfer to give effect to a Settlement under which the existing Registered Proprietor is the Tenant for Life, but the donees of an overriding power of appointment vested in him and another are to be registered as Proprietors.

(*Head and begin as in Form* 6 *down to* "*under which*") the land comprised in the title above referred to is limited to such uses as I, *A. B.* of etc., and *C. D.* of etc., shall jointly appoint, and subject thereto to various uses by virtue of which I am (*or* have the powers of) tenant for life under the Settled Land Acts, 1882 to 1890, I hereby transfer to myself and the said *C. D.* all the said land, and apply for the entry on the Register of the following inhibition (*fill in Form* 5).

FORM 8.

Instrument of Transfer by the representative of a deceased settlor, transferring the land to the Tenant for Life or to the Trustees.

(*Head and begin as in Form* 6 *down to* "*under which*") *A. B.* of etc. is (*or* has the powers of) tenant for life under the Settled Land Acts, 1882 to 1890, and *C. D.* of etc., and *E. F.* of etc., are the trustees for the purposes of the same Acts, I, *G. H.* of etc., with the consent of the said *A. B.* as tenant for life, hereby transfer to him (*or* to the said *C. D.* and *E. F.*) the land comprised in the title above referred to, and apply for the registration of the following restriction and inhibition (*fill in Form* 1 *or* 3, *as the case may be*).

FORM 9.

The like, where there is an overriding power of appointment.

(*Head and begin as in Form* 6 *down to* "*under which*") the land comprised in the title above referred to is limited to such uses as *A. B.* of etc., and *C. D.* of etc., shall jointly appoint, and subject thereto to various uses, by virtue of which the said *A. B.* is (*or* has the powers of) tenant for life under the Settled Land Acts, 1882 to 1890, *E. F.* of etc., with the consent of the said *A. B.* as tenant for life, hereby transfer to him and the said *C. D.* all the said land, and hereby apply for the entry on the Register of the following inhibition (*fill in Form* 5).

FORM 10.

Instrument of Transfer where registered land is purchased with capital moneys liable to be laid out in the purchase of land to be settled to the uses of a Settlement, the Tenant for life being registered as Proprietor.

(Heading as in Form 6.)

(*Date*) In consideration of £   paid out of capital moneys arising under a settlement (*etc. as in Form* 6 *down to* "*under which*") *A. B.* of

FORMS. 149

etc. is (*or* has the powers of) tenant for life under the Settled Land
Acts, 1882 to 1890, and *C. D.* of etc. and *E. F.* of etc. are the trustees
for the purposes of the same Acts, I, *G. H.* of etc. [*the vendor*], with
the consent of the said *A. B.*, hereby transfer to him all the land
comprised in the title above referred to, and we, the said *C. D.* and
E. F. hereby apply for the registration of the following restriction and
inhibition (*fill in Form* 1).

FORM 10

FORM 11.
The like—Trustees being registered as Proprietors.
(Heading as in Form 6.)

(*Date*) In consideration (*etc. as in last form down to and including
consent of* A. B.) hereby transfer to the said *C. D.* and *E. F.* all the
land (*etc., as in last Form, substituting restriction as in Form* 3).

FORM 12.
The like, where there is an overriding power of Appointment.
(Heading as in Form 6.)

(*Date*) In consideration (*etc., as in Form* 10 *down to* "*under which*"
and continue as in Form 9).

FORM 13.
Instrument of Charge by way of Annuity.
(Heading as in Form 6.)

(*Date*) I, *A. B.*, of etc., hereby charge the land (*a*) comprised in the
title above referred to with the payment to *C. D.*, of etc., of an annuity of
£   for   years (*or* during his life, etc.) payable (half-yearly,
quarterly, etc.), on the   of   etc., in every year.

NOTE.—If there is any consideration, it can be stated at the commencement, as :—" To secure £   part of the purchase money of
the land comprised in the title above referred to," or " In consideration
of an instrument of transfer of even date herewith of the land comprised
in the title above referred to," etc., etc.

(*a*.) If only part of the land comprised in the title is charged, add
here " shown and edged with red in the accompanying plan,
signed by me, being part of the land."

FORM 14.
Application to alter the terms of a Charge under Section 9 (5) of the Act of 1897.
(Heading as in Form 6.)

(*Date*) We, *A. B.*, of etc. [*registered proprietor of the land*], *C. D.*,
of etc. [*registered proprietor of the charge*], and *E. F.*, of etc. [*registered
proprietor of a charge of equal or inferior priority prejudicially affected*],
hereby apply to the Registrar to alter the terms of the charge dated
     of   18 , registered   of   18 , against title No.   ,
as follows :—
(*Fill in proposed alteration.*)

NOTE.—The application will be signed by *A. B.*, *C. D.*, and *E. F.*

FORM 15.

FORM 15.
Assent to a devise of land under Section 3 of the Act of 1897.

(Heading as in Form 6.)

(*Date*) I, *A. B.*, of etc., as executor of the late *C. D.*, of etc., hereby assent to the devise contained in the Will of the said *C. D.* to *E. F.* of the land comprised in the title above referred to.

(To be signed by *A. B.* and verified.)

NOTE.—If the assent is to be subject to a charge for payment of money which the executor is liable to pay, the form may be varied accordingly.

See also Note (*a*) to Form 13.

FORM 16.
Appropriation of Land in satisfaction of a Legacy or share in Residuary Estate under Section 4 of the Act of 1897.

Heading and commencement as in last Form down to "hereby," and then :—

With the consent of *E. F.* of etc., who is entitled to a legacy (*or* share in residuary estate) under the will of the said *C. D.*, appropriate to the said *E. F.* the land comprised in the title above referred to, and certify that all proper notices under the 4th section of the Land Transfer Act, 1897, have been given and the requirements of the rules of the Court in respect of the matter duly complied with.

(To be signed by *A. B.* and *E. F.* and verified.)

See also Note (*a*) to Form 13.

FORM 17.
Notice of Liability to Death Duty.

The land is liable to such death duties as may be payable or arise by reason of the death of *A. B.* of etc., who died on the   of   , 18   , *or* by reason of a settlement created by deed dated, etc., *or* by reason of the determination of a lease dated, etc., *or as the case may be.*

FORM 18.
Certificate of Non-liability to Death Duty.

This is to certify that the land (*or, if so*, shown and edged with red on the accompanying plan marked   , being part of the land) comprised in the title No.   , may be registered without notice of any liability to death duty by reason of the death of *A. B.*, of etc., and that any such notice already registered may be cancelled.

FORM 19.
Entry of no Survivorship of Joint Proprietors.

When the number of joint proprietors has been reduced to (one, two, etc.,) no registered disposition of the land (*or* charge) shall be made except under an order of the Court or an order of the Registrar, after an inquiry into title, subject to an appeal to the Court.

NOTE.—Copies of the Rules may be obtained at the Land Registry, Lincoln's Inn Fields.

INDEX.

ACCOUNT,
    liability of personal representatives to, 88.

ACT OF PARLIAMENT,
    definition of "land" in, 38.
    marginal notes are not part of, 21.

ACTIONS BY PERSONAL REPRESENTATIVES,
    before probate, 62, 63.

ADMINISTRATION,
    actions before, 63.
    agreement before, not enforceable, 63.
    creditors may claim, when, 17.
    heir, right of, to, 15, 16.
    separate, to real estate, court has power to grant, whether, 17.

ADMINISTRATOR,
    actions by, before grant, 63.
    assent by, of infant *durante minore ætate*, 104.
    executor of, cannot administer original estate, 18.
    heir, claim of, to be, 15, 16.
    interest of, equal to that of executor, 59.
    of administrator cannot administer original estate, 14, 18.
    of executor, sole or surviving, cannot administer original estate, 14.
    real estate of intestate vests in, 14.
    survival of office of, 18.
    time when real estate vests in, 18, 19.

AGENTS,
    employment of, by personal representatives, 87.

APPOINTMENT,
    Act of 1897, application of, to, 35.
    assent necessary to complete title under, 37.
    assets, when, 36, 37.
    general and particular powers of, distinguished, 35
    general gift, effect of, as to, 36.

APPROPRIATION OF REAL ESTATE,
    Act of 1897, power to make, under, 112—115.
                registration of proprietor claiming under, 117.
    former rule as to, 113.
    stamp duty on conveyance, 118.
    tenant for life, rights of, 115.

INDEX.

ASSENT,
    appointee of real estate cannot make good title before, 37.
    before probate, 62, 104.
    by whom, may be given, 103.
        by administrator *durante minore ætate*, 104.
        by married women, 104.
        by one of several executors, 103.
    conditional, 106.
    compellable after year from death, 109, 110.
    entry by executor on estate devised to him, effect of, 103.
    evidence of, what, may be required by purchasers, 107, 117.
    form of, none, prescribed except for registration, 108, 116, 117.
    implication of, from acts of executor, 107.
        from informal expressions, 107.
    jury, question is for, as to, 109.
    liability of executor giving, where debts unpaid, 105.
    necessity of, to complete title of appointee, 37.
        of devisee, 100.
    parol, 108.
    presumption of, after lapse of time, 108.
    recovery of possession, action for, after, 101.
    registration of devisee after, 116, 117.
    relation of, back to death of testator, 100.
    retraction of, 106.
    stamp duty on, 117.
    to devise, is assent to annexed condition, 102.
        of particular estate is assent to remainders, 102
    to residuary devise, 102.
    transmissible interest of devisee before, 100.

ASSETS,
    application of, order of, 93, 94,
    appointments under general powers, 36, 37.
    autre vie, estates *pur*, 2, 3, 35.
    charge of debts, effect of, under former law, 96, 97.
        under present law, 97.
    legal and equitable, distinction between, 94, 95.
        real estate is, in hands of personal representatives, 97.
    priority of payment of debts out of, 97, 98.
    proof, rules as to, 95.

BASE FEE,
    enlargement of, 28,

BENEFICE,
    nomination to, during period of administration, 42—44.

BREACH OF TRUST,
    jurisdiction to protect in case of innocent, 89.
    liability of personal representatives for, 86.

INDEX.

COMMISSION,
    personal representatives not allowed, 86.

COMMON LAW,
    devolution of real estate by, 1.

CONDITION,
    assent to devise is assent to annexed, 102.
        upon, 106.

CONTINGENT REMAINDER,
    application of Act of 1897 to real estate devised by way of, 50, 51.

CONVEYANCE TO HEIR OR DEVISEE,
    assent to devise, rights of purchasers before, to, 111.
        whether sufficient substitute for, 101.
    appropriation of real estate does not dispense with necessity for, 115.
    jurisdiction to compel, 110.
    married women may compel, 111.
    refusal to convey, grounds for, 111.
        liability for, 110.
    stamp duty on, 118.

COPARCENERS,
    exception of, from Act of 1897...23.

COPYHOLDS,
    admission to, saving of mortgagee's right to, 25.
    exception of, from Act of 1897, 24, 25.
    manor includes, 40.
    sale of, by executors, etc., for payment of debts, 69, 70.
    seignory includes freehold estates in, and rights over, 41.

CREDITORS,
    administration can be claimed by, whether, 17.
    priority of, as to payment out of assets, 97, 98.
        of specialty, abolished, 69.

CUSTOMARY FREEHOLDS,
    exception of, from Act of 1897...24, 25.
    seignory includes freehold of, 41.

DEBTS,
    charge of, effect of, under former law, 96.
    payment of, assent before, 83, 84.
        contingent, provision for, 82, 83.
        liability of personal representatives to see to, 82.
        priority of, out of assets, 97, 98. *See* ASSETS.
        real estate formerly not liable to, 67.

DEVISE,
    assent to, 99, *et seq. And see* ASSENT,
    settlement created by, effect of, 55—58.
    Statute of Uses, 1.
    Wills Act, 2.

INDEX.

DISTRESS,
    before probate, 62.
    power of personal representatives to levy, 78.

DUTY,
    liability of real estate to, 118, 119.

EASEMENTS,
    vesting of, in personal representatives, 45, 46.

ENTRY,
    assent to devise not implied by, of executors on land devised to hi 103.
    before probate, 61.
    rights of, devolve on personal representatives, whether, 47, 48.

EQUITABLE INTERESTS IN LAND,
    devolution of, on personal representatives, 21, 22.

ESTATE DUTY,
    provisions of Act of 1897, as to, 118, 119.

ESTATE FOR LIFE,
    determination of, by death, lets in remainderman, 33.
    tenant for life, powers of, under Settled Land Acts, 55—58.
        rights of, under appropriation, 115.

ESTATE IN FEE SIMPLE,
    devolution of, on personal representatives, 26, 27.

ESTATE, PUR AUTRE VIE,
    assets in hands of heir, when, 2, 3, 35.
    devolution of, by Wills Act, where no special occupant, 2.
        on heir as special occupant not affected, 33—35.

ESTATE TAIL,
    barrable by actual tenant in tail, 31.
            by personal representatives, whether, 31, 32.
            by trustee of bankrupt tenant in tail, 30 n.
            concurrence of tenant in tail renders, 32.
    base fee, enlargement of, 28.
    devolution of, on personal representatives of deceased tenant in tail, 27, 28.
    nature and incidents of, 27.
    Settled Land Acts, powers of sale, etc., under, 28, 29.
    surplus proceeds of sale, etc., of, destination of, 31, 32.

EVIDENCE,
    of appropriation of real estate to legacies, etc., 117.
    of assent to devise, 107, 117.

EXECUTOR,
    administrator, interest of, equal to that of, 59.
            of sole or surviving, cannot administer original estate, 14.
    assent by, 99 *et seq.* *And see* ASSENT.

INDEX.

Executors,
    of administrator cannot administer original estate, 18.
    of sole or surviving, vesting of real estate in, 13.
    separate, of real and personal estate, 11—13.
    survival of office of, 13.
    time when real estate devolves on, 18.

Executory Devise,
    application of Act of 1897 to real estate devised by way of, 50.

Fee Farm Rent,
    vesting of, in personal representatives, 44.

Fraudulent Devises Acts,
    actions against heirs and devisees for ancestor's debts under, 67, 68.

Heir,
    administration to real estate, claims to, of, 15, 16.
    devolution by common law of real estate on, 1.
        under Act of 1897 considered, 84—86.

Husband,
    claim of, to administration of wife's personal estate, 15—16.

Incorporeal Hereditaments,
    vesting of, in personal representatives, 40—46.

Infant,
    assent cannot be given by, 104.
    Settled Land Acts, exercise of powers of, on behalf of, 57.

Joint Tenancy,
    exception of, from Act of 1897...23.
    severance of, 23.

Jury,
    assent is question for, 109.

Land,
    definition of, in Act of 1897...38.
        in Acts of Parliament generally, 38.
    vesting of, in personal representatives, 38, 39.

Land Transfer Act, 1875,
    personal representative of bare trustee intestate, vesting of registered lands in, 3.
    personal representative of proprietor of registered charge, power of to transfer or reconvey mortgage, 3.

INDEX.

LAND TRANSFER ACT, 1897,
 application of Part I., general, 8.
 commencement of, 6.
 coparceners, 23.
 effect of, general, 5, 6.
  particular. *See* TABLE OF CONTENTS.
 interpretation of terms in joint tenants, 23.
 preamble to, 9.
 title of, 5, 9.
  And see APPENDIX, pp. 121 *et seq.*

LEASES BY PERSONAL REPRESENTATIVES,
 before probate, 62.
 concurrence of devisee or heir in, advisable, 77, 78.
 contract by deceased owner for, 77.
 demise for term of years whether allowable, 76, 77.
  from year to year allowable, 76.
 option to purchase must not be given, 77.
 repairing leases, 77.
 to corporation, 77.

LEGACIES,
 annuities are, 113, n.
 appropriation of real estate to, 112—115.
 real estate whether subject to, under Act of 1897...92 93.
  And see NOTE TO PREFACE, p. vii.

LEGAL ESTATE,
 devolution of, on personal representatives, 20.
 outstanding in mortgagee, 22.
  in trustees, 21.

MANAGEMENT OF REAL ESTATE,
 distress for rent, 78.
 duty as to, for benefit of persons entitled, 86.
 express provisions as to, advisability of, 81.
 leases, 75—77. *See* LEASES.
 mines and minerals, working, 79.
 repairs and improvements, 79.
  liability under lessor's covenant for, 79.
 timber, felling, 80.
 trade or business, employment of real estate in, 80, 81.

MANOR,
 Act of 1897, devolution of, on personal representatives of, 40—42.
 copyholds, included in, 40.

MARRIED WOMAN,
 assent by, 104.
 conveyance by personal representatives compellable by, 111.
 husband's right to administration of personal estate of, 15, 16.

MINES,
 sale of, apart from surface, 72.
 working of, by personal representatives, 79, 80.

INDEX.

MORTGAGE BY PERSONAL REPRESENTATIVES,
    application of mortgage moneys, liability to see to, 74.
    before probate, 61, 62.
    interest, rate of, 74.
    power of, implied from power to sell, 65.
        under Lord St. Leonard's Act, 66.
    power of sale may be given to mortgagee, 73, 74.
    under charge of debts, 64, 65.
        express powers, 64.
        Land Transfer Act, 1897...69, 73, 74.
        Lord St. Leonard's Act, 66.

MORTGAGE ESTATES,
    devolution of, on death, 3, 4.

MORTGAGEE,
    admission of, to copyholds, 25.
    legal estate outstanding in, 22.

NEXT-OF-KIN,
    right of, to administration, 16, 17.

NEW RIVER SHARES,
    vesting of, in personal representatives, 45.

PERSONAL ESTATE,
    administration to, right of creditor to, 17.
            husband to, 15, 16.
            next-of-kin to, 16.
    devolution of, on death, 1, 2.

PERSONAL REPRESENTATIVES,
    account, liability to, of, 88.
    actions by, before probate or administration, 62, 63.
    advowson vests in, 42—44. *See* ADVOWSON.
    agents, employment of, by, 87.
    appropriation of real estate to legacies, etc., 112—115.
    assent to devises, 99 *et seq. See* ASSENT.
    assets, order of application of, by, 93, 94.
        real estate is legal, in hands of, 97.
    breach of trust, liability for, of, 86.
            statutory protection in respect of, 89.
    commission for trouble not allowed to, 86.
    conveyance to devisee or heir by, 110, 111.
    devolution on, of base fee, 28.
            of easements, 45, 46.
            of fee farm rents, 45.
            of equitable interests in land, 21, 22.
            of estate in fee, 27.
            pur autre vie, 2, 33—35.
            tail, 27, 28.
            of rights of entry, 47, 48.
    distress by, 62, 78.
    duration of interest of, 59.
    leases by, 75—77.
    legal estate vests in, 20.

INDEX.

PERSONAL REPRESENTATIVES—*continued.*
    management of estate by, 78 *et seq.* *See* MANAGEMENT.
    manor vests in, 40—42.
    mines, working of, by, 79, 80.
    mortgages by, 61, 62, 74.
    mortgage estates vest in, 3, 4.
    nature of interest of, 52—59.
    personal estate vests in, 1, 2.
    probate or administration, dealings before by, 60—63.
    profits *à prendre* vest in, 46.
    quantity of estate vesting in, 25—35.
    real estate of deceased owner vests in, 14.
        time of vesting of, 18, 19.
    registration of, 117.
    rentcharges vest in, 44, 45.
    repairs by, 79.
    sales by, 61, 62, 71—74. *And see* SALE.
    survival of office of, 13, 14, 18.
    timber, felling of, by, 80.
    time when real estate vests in, 18, 19.
    tithes vest in, 44.
    trade, carrying on, by, 80, 81.
    trust estates vest in, 3, 4.
    vesting of personal estate in, 2, 3.
        of real estate in, 9.
    waste, liability for, of, 87.

POWERS,
    of appointment, distinction between general and special, 35.
    of appropriation under Act of 1897...112—117.

PROBATE,
    dealings with real estate before, 60—62.
        actions by personal representatives, 62, 63.
        distress, 62.
        entry, 61.
    death of executor before, 62.
    of real estate, where no personal estate, 10.

PROFITS A PRENDRE,
    vesting of, in personal representatives, 46.

REAL ESTATE,
    administration to, separate, 17.
    appropriation of, to legacies, etc., 112—115.
    common law, devolution by, of, 1.
    contingent remainders, 50, 51.
    debts of ancestor formerly not payable out of, 67.
    definition of, in Act of 1897, now given, 37.
    devises of, statutes enabling, 1.
    devolution of, by common law, 1.
    duty, liability to, of, 118, 119.
    probate of, where no personal estates, 10.
    registration of, 116, 117.
    sale of, under powers, express, 64.
                   implied by charge of debts, etc., 64, 65.

INDEX.

REAL ESTATE—*continued*.
    vesting of, in personal representatives, 14.
    what, will devolve by Act of 1897—
        advowsons, 42—44.
        easements, 45, 46.
        fee farm rents, 45.
        land, 39, 40.
        manors, 40, 42.
        New River shares, 45.
        profits *à prendre*, 46.
        rentcharges, 44, 45.
    what, will not devolve by Act of 1897—
        rights of entry, 47, 48.
        titles of honour, 46, 47.

REAL REPRESENTATIVES,
    establishment of,
        Act of 1897, affirms desirability of, 9.
            does not effect, 9.
        court has no power to order, 9.
        testamentary, would contravene the Act, 9.

REGISTRATION,
    by personal representatives, 117.
    form prescribed for, of appropriation, 117.
            of assent, 108, 116, 117.

REMAINDER,
    assent to, is assent to particular devise and *vice versâ*, 102.
    contingent, 50, 51.

RENTCHARGE,
    vesting of, in personal representatives, 44.

REPAIRS,
    application of rents, etc., for, 79.
    covenants by lessee for, leases in consideration of, 77.
        by lessor for, liability under, 79.

RIGHTS OF ENTRY,
    devolution of, 47, 48,

SALE,
    application of purchase money, liability to see to, 74.
    before probate, 61, 62.
    benefit of persons entitled should be considered, 72.
    by auction or private contract, 71.
    by court, where no power in executors, 67.
    depreciatory conditions, 73.
    incumbrances, provision for discharge of, on, 72.
    necessity for, purchaser need not inquire into, 90.
            rights of heir or devisee where no, 91.
    of copyholds by executors, etc., for payment of debts, 69, 70
    of mines and surface separately, 72.
    of timber and land separately, 72.
    powers of, express, 64.
        implied by charges of debts, etc., 64—66.
        under Lord St. Leonard's Act, 66, 67.
        under Act of 1897.. 69—74.
    valuation should be made before, 72, 73.

INDEX.

Seignory,
incidents of, 41.

Settled Land Acts,
powers of tenant for life, by whom exerciseable during period of administration under, 55—58.

Shifting Uses,
application of Act of 1897 to real estate devised by way of, 49.

Stamp Duty,
appropriation of real estate to legacies, etc., 118.
assent, 117.

Succession Duty,
liability under Act of 1897 as to, 119.

Timber,
power of personal representatives to cut, 80.
sale of, apart from land, 72.

Time,
assent presumed after lapse of, 108.
real estate vests in personal representatives, at what, 18.

Tithes,
devolution of, on personal representatives, 44.

Title,
assent necessary to complete, of appointee, 37.
of devisee, 100.
of honour, devolution of, 46.

Trader,
carrying on business of, by personal representatives, 80, 81.

Trust Estates,
devolution of, under Conveyancing Act, 1881...3, 4.
exception of, from Act of 1897...24.

Trustees,
legal estate outstanding in, 21.
personal representatives are, 52, 58.

Vendor and Purchaser Act, 1874,
mortgagee, personal representatives might convey legal estate under, 3.

Waste,
liability of personal representatives for, 87.

Will,
appointments by, of real estate, 35—37.
devisability of real estate by, 1.

www.ingramcontent.com/pod-product-compliance
Lightning Source LLC
Chambersburg PA
CBHW022112160426
43197CB00009B/995